C000260153

THE WAY TO TRADE

Discover your
successful
trading personality

JOHN PIPER

HARRIMAN HOUSE LTD

3A Penns Road
Petersfield
Hampshire
GU32 2EW
GREAT BRITAIN

Tel: +44 (0)1730 233870
Fax: +44 (0)1730 233880
Email: enquiries@harriman-house.com
Website: www.harriman-house.com

First published in Great Britain in 1999
reprinted by Harriman House 2006 & 2009
Copyright © Harriman House Ltd

Foreword © Alexander Elder 1999

The right of John Piper to be identified as author has been asserted
in accordance with the Copyright, Design and Patents Act 1988.

ISBN: 978-1-897597-94-1

British Library Cataloguing in Publication Data
A CIP catalogue record for this book can be obtained from the British Library.

All rights reserved; no part of this publication may be reproduced, stored in a retrieval
system, or transmitted in any form or by any means, electronic, mechanical,
photocopying, recording, or otherwise without the prior written permission of the
Publisher. This book may not be lent, resold, hired out or otherwise disposed of by
way of trade in any form of binding or cover other than that in which it is published
without the prior written consent of the Publisher.

Printed and bound by the CPI Group, Antony Rowe.

No responsibility for loss occasioned to any person or corporate body acting
or refraining to act as a result of reading material in this book can be
accepted by the Publisher, by the Author, or by the employer of the Author.

About the Author

John Piper has been involved with markets since his early twenties. In the late 1980s he started to trade options full time and did so right through the Crash of 1987 – an experience that stands him in good stead for markets today. For over a decade he has been the editor of *The Technical Trader*, the leading newsletter in the UK for those who trade futures and options markets worldwide. His articles bring a fine edge of analysis to markets and how they work. He trades full time, making consistent profits, and now manages money for selected clients at Berkeley Futures Limited, a firm regulated by the SFA. He lives in Cobham, Surrey and in Massa, Italy.

This book is dedicated to
all those who are struggling with markets, whoever and
wherever they may be.

CONTENTS

Why you need this book   xi

Foreword by Dr Alexander Elder   xv

Introduction   xvii

Acknowledgements   xix

Section 1
THE UNDERLYING PHILOSOPHY

1 An introduction to the Trading Pyramid   3

The Trading Pyramid   4

Summary   9

2 The evolution of a trader and the 55 steps   11

The three stages   12

The 55 steps (a personal journey to success)   15

Summary   19

3 The human brain   21

Structure of the brain   22

Trading chaos   26

Summary   26

4 You – the first level of the pyramid and why   29

The trading experience   30

Summary   33

5 Commitment   35

The nature of the market   35

Market Profile   37

Summary   39

6 Discipline   41

Discipline and the Trading Pyramid   42

System parameters 43
Summary 45

7 Money Management 47

Using Money Management 48
Position size 49
Monitoring position 50
Summary 51

8 Risk control 53

Risk inherent in the vehicle 54
Risk inherent in the market 55
Other forms of risk 55
Summary 57

9 The three simple rules (or trading secrets) 59

The trading secrets 60
Following the rules 61
Summary 66

10 System parameters – the thinking behind system design 67

Buying options 68
Writing options 68
Futures 68
Designing a system 69
Summary 75

11 System parameters – simple trading rules and the human brain 77

Systems 78
The human brain 79
Summary 81

12 Developing your methodology 83

Time frame 84
Trading type 84
Analysis type 85
Money Management (MM) 85
Risk control (RC) 87
Entry methodology (EM) 87

Exit methodology (ExM)   87
Interview with an institutional trader   88
Summary   93

13 Operation   95

The set-up   96
Problems with operation   97
Summary   99

14 The whole structure = profit/loss   101

Summary   103

15 Stops and acceptance   105

Are stops necessary?   105
Stop approaches   106
Acceptance   107
Summary   110

16 A trading coach?   111

The benefits of working with a coach   111
Adrienne Toghraie   113
First steps   114
Summary   115

Section 2
MARKET TECHNIQUES AND METHODOLOGIES

17 Some points of principle   119

More general points   120
Low risk trading opportunities   122
Trading tips   123
Summary   125

18 Market Profile and Minus Development   127

Market Profile   127
Minus Development   130
Value   130
Other concepts   132
TTT article   132
Trading tips with Market Profile   136
Summary   137

19 Futures and options 139

Stocks 139
Futures 140
Options 141
Summary 149

20 Spiky action 151

Trading Trend 151
Types of spike 152
Summary 153

21 An options strategy 155

The options strategy – principle 155
The options strategy – operation 157
Options – the hedging strategy 158
Summary 163

22 A number of futures strategies 165

Gas opens – code word: goose 166
Failed breakthroughs – code word: goat 169
Failed re-tests – code word: snake 172
Square congestion – code word: box 172
Key levels – code word: piano 173
Eliott fives – code word: illusion 174
Aborted patterns – code word: platypus 175
Trend following – code word: horse 176
Corrective action 177
Other systemized approaches 178
Summary 179

23 Systems 181

Stops 182
One secret to success 183
A few additional comments 183
My own trading 183
My trading rules 184
Risk warning/disclaimer 185

It doesn't end here   186
Summary   187

24 Trading systems and when to use them   189

Trading systems   189
How to make a fortune trading futures   191
Summary   193

25 Market myths   195

Indicators and market techniques   195
News   196
Zero sum? Don't you believe it!   196
Systems   197
Summary   197

26 The 10-step approach to futures and options trading   199

Step   1: Where am I now?   199
Step   2: Where do I want to go?   200
Step   3: Survival (1)   200
Step   4: Survival (2)   201
Step   5: Methodologies   201
Step   6: Theory   202
Step   7: Practice   203
Step   8: Fear   203
Step   9: Running profits   204
Step 10: Expertise   204
The consultancy service   204
Summary   205

Section 3
A CHART TUTORIAL

27 Low risk trading opportunities on U.S. and U.K. markets   209

Section 4
AN OPTIONS TRADING CAMPAIGN

28 A war of attrition   221

Epilogue   231

APPENDICES

1 **Follow-up Services**   239
2 **The Troubled Trader** by Tony Plummer, MSTA   241
3 **Recommended reading**   255
4 **Trading and psychology questionnaire**   257
5 **Is Elliott addictive?**   269

The Fortune Strategy   275

Index   285

WHY YOU NEED THIS BOOK

If you are an individual trader, whether a novice or experienced, you will benefit from reading this book because:

1 Trading the futures and options markets leads to a greater compounding of wealth than any other method available. Billions have been made in days on many occasions, and will be made again. Nothing else comes close.

2 It is possible to make money in the markets *consistently*. It is possible to beat the market. The author, John Piper, among many others, has done it. To do the same you need to follow a proven methodology which suits your personality. This book explains how.

3 This book also sets out a number of proven methodologies, giving you a head start in selecting the one which will work for you.

4 But it also goes a lot further. John Piper wrote this book because he had never come across a book which deals with the whole issue of trading. There are many books which deal with market analysis, and technical analysis techniques. There are many books which deal with psychology. There are books which deal with money management and all manner of other subjects, some even cover a range of topics. But no other book covers it all, from a successful philosophy of trading, through all the psychology, into the methodologies, the operation thereof, and the end result.

5 It is rare to find a book which appreciates that it is no good doing it "how I say." We each have to find our own route to success. This book spells out why that is, and how to do it. That is what *The Way to Trade* is all about.

6 The futures and options markets offer the biggest potential for growth, far more than is offered by stock markets. The people who really make it big do so in these markets. Perhaps more importantly you can make money whether markets go up or down. In coming years this may be important.

Fascinated? You should be, and anyone who is into money, and wants lots more of it should check out this book. Rich or poor, working or retired, there is something for everyone in these pages.

Why this book is unique

Trading is a life experience, it is not like any other business. As you become a better trader, you become a better person. But as you evolve it is difficult to look back at where you were. I believe this is why there are no other books which cover all the ground. Those traders who do make it often "forget" how they got there, not surprisingly, as a lot of the skills become subconscious.

However, John has always combined his trading with writing about markets. This has given him a fairly unique insight and forced him to express personal matters which other traders just assume. It has also forced him to more carefully examine the precise process involved in becoming a successful trader. It is solely through this process that John Piper "discovered" the Trading Pyramid. This is the first attempt to create a model for trading success and traders will find it immensely useful.

So not only does this book take the trader right through from the beginning to the end result (trading profits, lots of them!) it also provides a framework against which to work.

There are no right or wrong ways to trade

The only thing that counts is the result. This book sets out a range of parameters within which to build the system that suits you. The beauty of trading is that it becomes an expression of your own personality. Good traders don't do, they simply are. But to become a good trader you have got to find the approach which will work for you. This book, and the follow-up services that are available with it, will help you do just that.

Follow your own path

But to get there you must follow your own path. It is no good following the trades other people do. Certainly you need help to learn this business, which is what this book is all about. You need a mentor, but you do not need gurus who tell you how to trade. You will only win by trading your way.

Indeed Frank Sinatra's big hit "My Way" is an excellent anthem for any trader. Taking that step to do it by yourself is one many traders find the most difficult, but it is essential.

If you don't want to do it your way then you are better off giving your money to another trader, like John Piper, so that he can trade it for you. But make sure you check out the track record and risk profile first.

FOREWORD

by Dr Alexander Elder
Financial Trading Inc.

Successful trading is based on 3 Ms – Mind, Method, Money.

Mind refers to your trading psychology. You must follow certain psychological rules that lead to winning when faithfully applied and avoid pitfalls that become death traps for most losers.

Method refers to how you find your trades – how you decide what to buy or sell. Each trader needs a method for choosing specific stocks, options, or futures as well as rules for "pulling the trigger" – deciding exactly when to buy and sell.

Money refers to how you manage your trading capital. You may have a brilliant trading system, but if your Money Management is poor, you are guaranteed to lose money. A single unlucky trade can destroy your account if Money Management is not in place.

Trading psychology, trading method, and Money Management – people sometimes ask me which of the three is most important. I answer – imagine sitting on a three-legged stool. It is pretty stable, but try getting comfortable sitting on that stool after taking away any one of its three legs. Now please tell me which of the three legs is most important?

Traders go through three stages of development. When people first approach the markets, they usually focus on the method. Most of them do not survive this stage. They are too inexperienced and do not have anyone who can tell them how to stay out of trouble. No amount of optimized moving averages or fine-tuned trendlines will keep them alive in the markets.

Those who survive that stage acquire a greater sense of confidence. They acquire a method of selecting what to trade and the tools for analyzing markets and deciding when to buy or sell. Some become quite proficient in technical analysis, market indicators and systems, using computers to search on-line databases. Then the smarter survivors start asking themselves: if I am so good, how come I am making so little money? How come my account is up 20 per cent one month, and down 20 per cent or worse the next month? I clearly know something about the markets – why can't I hold on to what I make?

Traders at the second stage tend to grab profits and buy something before their money evaporates in a series of bad trades. Then one day they look in a mirror and realize that the biggest obstacle to winning is the person they see in it. Impulsive and undisciplined trades with no protective stops lead to losses. A trader who survives the second stage comes to recognize that his or her personality, with all its complexes, quirks, and faults is just as much a trading tool as the computer.

Traders who survived that stage become more relaxed, quieter, not jumpy in the markets. They are now in the third stage – focusing on managing money in their trading accounts. Their trading system is in place, they are at peace with themselves, and they spend more and more time thinking how to allocate their trading capital in order to reduce overall risks.

The concept of the 3 M's comes from my book *Trading for a Living* which has become an international bestseller. I met John Piper six years ago and enjoyed watching him grow and mature as a trader and a teacher of traders. It gives me pleasure to see that we share a number of ideas about markets, such as the 2% Rule, the concept of the market as a manifestation of human psychology, buying below value and selling above value, the market as a minus-sum game.

In the book you are about to read John Piper takes you beyond theory in a very useful Chart Tutorial. He invites you to follow him through a series of trades, commenting on his actions along the way. He provides an essential lesson that most beginners never get.

In *The Way to Trade* John Piper mentions that he has been managing money profitably for the past year and I know that he has been trading for many years before that. To get really serious money under management in the US requires a five year audited track record. I wish John success in continuing to make consistent profits and his readers a captivating and profitable journey into the financial markets.

Dr Alexander Elder
New York – Moscow, November 1998

INTRODUCTION

I have been trading futures and options markets for over a decade. I now manage money and make good consistent profits. So what I have to say about markets has been forged in the fire of market action itself. I have suffered the highs and the lows which all traders experience on the road to success.

This book is unique in that it takes the reader right through the trading process and it also uses a model, the trading pyramid, which explains the process and the inter-relation between the component parts.

The key component for successful trading is the underlying philosophy of trading and this is what so many books and seminars ignore. There is so much written and spoken about analysis but that is such a small part of the game. *Good trading is not a question of doing, it is a question of being.* This book is dedicated to those who want to become good traders. *Analysis and trading technique are useless to those who have not gone through this process.*

Having dealt with the underlying philosophy, we then move onto specific trading techniques and the underlying analysis which builds those techniques. I do not believe that analysis is used correctly by the vast majority of those who risk capital in worldwide markets. Analysis is not for use on markets, it is solely to devise your methodology/ approach to the market. You must devise this methodology and then use it. Thus you become an expert in its application and then the money flows your way.

But you must have your own methodology; it is no good being spoon fed something by the currently "hot" guru. This is very unlikely to suit your trading personality. This book tells you how to develop your own methodology and explains the feedback process within the pyramid that will make it work for you.

Most people lose in the markets for one simple reason – they trade emotionally. When traders understand the problem they improve by becoming mechanical. This is a big improvement but it is still not enough. To be truly successful you have to become intuitive, and this simply means you become an expert in what you do – something you achieve through experience. It is this path I chart in this book. I think you will enjoy it.

Don't accept anything in this book at face value. It is an essential part of a trader's development to carefully consider all aspects of the market and his individual approach to it. Some of the statements made in this book are deliberately provocative and designed to ferment that process. So don't accept anything, think about it, draw your own conclusions, and thus create your own *useful* beliefs about markets and your methodology. The key word is 'useful'; your beliefs and techniques must prove their usefulness in producing lots of lovely profits.

Finally I must say that there are various lessons in trading which become particularly relevant at particular times during our progress towards success. For this reason you may find that parts of this book do not seem relevant to you the first time you read it. But they may well do so on a subsequent reading. This is a book which may repay frequent readings!

John Piper
December 1998

(Editor's note: *John welcomes comments on this book and contact details appear on page 240.*)

ACKNOWLEDGEMENTS

Many, many people have gone into the making of this book. Frequently I speak to a consultancy client or discuss a point with an attendee at one of my seminars and gain insight which I have tried to distill into these pages.

I am also grateful to the authors of the many works on markets and trading which I have read. The key works are listed in Appendix 3, but I must single out Tony Plummer whose article "The Troubled Trader" appears in Appendix 2. This article makes it clear why we find trading a tough proposition.

In my own trading career I owe a great deal to Adrienne Toghraie for her help with my psychology, and to Adam Seccombe who is, even now, helping bring in further sums for me to manage.

Thank you to those who took the trouble to read the first draft of this book, especially Dr Alexander Elder who was kind enough to also write the Foreword.

Thank you, also, to the team at Financial Times Pitman Publishing who are responsible for the work you hold in your hands, particularly Richard Stagg, Iain Campbell, Elizabeth Truran and Heather Serjeant.

Thanks also to my family who bore the brunt of the difficult years before I learnt how to make money consistently.

Finally I must thank Karen for all her help with the book, not the least for soothing my troubled brow when I most needed it.

Section 1

THE UNDERLYING PHILOSOPHY

Chapter 1

AN INTRODUCTION TO THE TRADING PYRAMID

When we enter the trading arena we enter an environment unlike anywhere else. The rules we have lived by in the normal outside world no longer apply and, indeed, will cause us loss. Our very motivation can be our own worst enemy as we seek to extract money from the markets.

To succeed in the markets we need to put in place an entire structure, as we have put in place an entire structure (personality) in the outside world. The Trading Pyramid is just such a structure. But before I begin to explain how it works let me give you two examples of why our normal behavior and motivations are not going to help us in the markets.

Many people enter the markets because they have had a successful career or business life elsewhere. At this point they may feel a little bored with life and seek a new challenge. This is very normal, and the kind of stimulus all of us have felt at one time or another. But think about this for a minute. Such an individual, starting to trade, will probably, like many other traders, trade in a fairly haphazard manner to start with. I term such trading "emotional," because whatever method traders may think they are using, the ultimate decision is more usually an emotional one. I will explain this in more detail later in this book. So the overall rationale can be described as "the person is bored and wants to trade." So what happens the next time boredom sets in? Once able to trade, it is very likely that a person will make the emotional decision to do just that when bored. This timing is unlikely to correspond with a low risk trading opportunity; I will also be talking a lot about those later in this book.

So the first question traders must ask themselves is "Why do I trade?" The answer to that simple question may save you a fortune.

Now to the second example. In this modern world where we all seek gratification as and when we want it, what do we do when we are offered something nice? We take it. In the real world what do we do when something unpleasant comes along? We seek to defer it and hope that time may lessen its impact. What are these tendencies going to do in the market? They are going to mean you take profits too quickly and take losses too slowly. Yes, you will be cutting your profits and running your losses. What works in the real world does *not* work in the market. These are just two of the many reasons why all traders need the Trading Pyramid.

The Trading Pyramid

The Trading Pyramid is illustrated in Figure 1.1. Each level builds on the next and, indeed, is essential if the next level is going to be put in place. Each trader already has such a structure in place but if trading and losing then the pyramid needs to be re-built along the right lines – lines which are going to be fully explained in this book.

In this chapter my only aim is to introduce the overall concept and in succeeding chapters I will look at each level in detail. The first level is *you*. Obviously if you are not in place, do not exist, then it will not be possible to add further levels. But also *you* determine the overall structure, as you have to build something which suits your overall personality. As such, each

> **You must learn to initiate and manage your own trades, nothing else is going to work.**

individual trader will have a somewhat different structure, although I believe there will always be common features. Because of this, it is vital that traders each plough their own field. I often tell my consultancy clients that one of the major steps they must take is to learn to be disinterested in what I or anyone else says about the market. Because your trading structure is going to be different from mine or from anyone else's you must learn to initiate and manage your own trades, nothing else is going to work. So already we can see how this model becomes useful – it gives us insights into the way trading works.

The next level is commitment. Trading is a tough business, in my

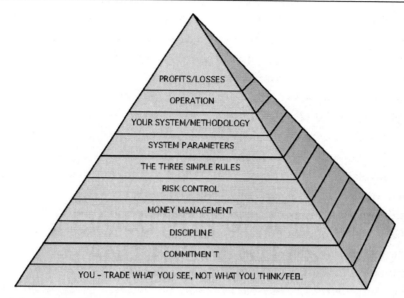

Fig 1.1   The Trading Pyramid

view one of the toughest. And that is only right as it is also the highest paid in the world for the high flyers – so you would expect it to be tough. If you are going to battle your way through then you are going to need to be committed. But even if you get as far as reading this book then you are probably already committed. That means that you have already accepted that it is not going to be easy.

Next comes discipline, a key factor in trading markets. You have to learn about your own emotions and control them. This takes discipline. You need to develop a methodology that gives you an edge, and if you are going to use that you will need the discipline to do so. This brings in another point, because there are some things we can do and some we cannot. We do not need to make it unduly difficult for ourselves, so our methodology should be one to which we are suited, it should also be one in which we become expert. Once these two conditions are in place the ability to exercise discipline and to follow our systems becomes a lot easier, although the discipline itself remains essential. But this is an example of how the various levels of the pyramid inter-relate. Also this illustrates how the structure is organic and evolves as our trading skills and experience grows. Our methodology is, in part, a function of our experiences of different market strategies and our knowledge about ourselves and our own emotions. So as we (*you*) evolve, this creates a feedback loop to our system/methodology which also has an impact on the discipline level, and all other levels.

We have so far looked at the first three levels and these levels may be categorized as the "Personal" levels; they contain what we bring to the party. For the purposes of these three levels, we may never have looked at markets, may never have taken a trade. The next five levels have to do with developing our methodology. There are many books on trading which only deal with system design. Some only deal with analysis techniques – yet this is a tiny part of this game, forming merely part of one of the levels within the pyramid – that level being System Parameters.

Money Management (MM) is the first key feature of any methodology. Without appropriate MM policies nothing is going to work. A system with a 99 per cent success rate (which sadly does not exist other than in the physical sciences, an airplane with that success rate would not be very popular!) would still wipe you out if you risked 100 per cent of your capital on each trade. Similarly risking too little on such a system would produce much less than you might otherwise expect. Getting your risk parameters right is the first step, and this also has to be personalized. Most people fail because they put themselves under too much pressure, this produces excess emotion, and emotional trading is a losing occupation. There are two types of pressure of particular importance. The first is financial pressure; if you risk too much cash then you become "a fugitive from the law of averages", and you will be wiped out, that is guaranteed. The second is psychological pressure, maybe as a subconscious realization of the financial pressure. Both of these must be avoided. Partly this has to do with experience, and partly with your risk parameters for each trade. I think that 1–2 per cent per trade is about right. You can still make lots of money but you need not feel pressurized. One of the "market wizards" said that almost all traders should immediately halve their trading size, that is good advice.

Next we have Risk Control (RC). MM and RC are interlinked. MM is essential, as set out above, but often MM policies include RC. For example using a stop loss point (mental or "in the market") controls risk, but the amount of risk is an MM matter. To be a successful trader you must minimize risk. It is for this reason that we often see sharp moves after a news item, often in the opposite direction to that suggested by the news item itself. This is because the big traders, who got that way by minimizing risk, wait for such risky items as news to be out of the way before taking positions. But what the news actually says is rarely of import – See Chapter 25 on Market Myths. Higher risk times include around news items, overnight and over the weekend, among others. Unexpected news items are something we can do nothing about except minimize risk at all times. We can never eliminate risk and we don't really want to because without the risk there would be no reward. Traders have to be like tightrope walkers. Many people think that tightrope walkers learn to balance, but they don't. Instead they learn to live with imbalance, in the same way a trader must learn to live with risk.

> *Traders have to be like tightrope walkers, they learn to live with imbalance, in the same way a trader must learn to live with risk.*

This takes us to the three simple rules, which I often call "trading secrets." You see the best place to hide anything is out in the open where everyone can see it. You see such things all the time but do not realize their value. This is completely true of the three simple rules. You know these well:

1. Cut your losses.
2. Run your profits.
3. Trade selectivity.

These correspond with the three stages which traders go through, although these stages can be described in different ways. The Evolution of a Trader (see Chapter 2) describes these three stages as "greed-orientated," "fear-orientated," and "risk-orientated." These three stages can be linked to the three simple rules. Another way of describing the trading experience can also be linked to three simple rules. This is Emotional to Mechanical to Intuitive, but we are getting a little ahead of ourselves. In my view any methodology which does not follow the three simple rules is not going to be effective. Having said that, some purely mechanical approaches are reputed to do well, but they would perform much better if you get the trade selectivity right (see again Chapter 25). Only now do we get to talk about market analysis, as we must now look at system parameters. But all the key features are already in place, and once they are in place we will have no real difficulty with system parameters because we will better know ourselves, know how we want to trade, know what we need to trade that way (rather than merely buying the software package with the glossiest brochure or the best sales pitch), and be able to do so – and this final stage should not be minimized.

In my opinion the purpose of analysis is generally misunderstood. It is not for market analysis, it is for putting your system in place. You must decide how you want to trade; futures, options, hedging, long term, short term, are all factors which relate to this. You may decide that you want to trade with the trend and hold trades for between three days and three weeks depending on market conditions. You may decide that some form of trend indicator would be useful within your approach. Alternatively you may prefer to observe market action and draw appropriate conclusions from that, as I do. But whichever style you adopt you need to decide what triggers you into a trade and also how to get out. Personally I leave some of this to intuition, but I am far from perfect in this. But the point I am making is that there is some flexibility at this stage and the key thing is that the system/methodology follows the principles laid down in all the stages of the pyramid up to this point, that it is in accord with your trading personality and what you are trying to achieve.

Once this is the case you have your system and it merely comes down to operation. Now the real problems can start. There is a trader in the USA called Joe Ross. Among many other things, he has said **"Trade what you see, not what you think."** This is the key phrase when it comes to operation. So many trades are taken because traders become convinced of what might happen, they imagine the riches which would flow from that big fall, or that big rally. *Wisdom lies in sticking with what you can see.*

Some traders develop blocks on their trading. I will deal with this in Chapter 13 on Operation. But to introduce this topic, some of these problems have to do with complex thought processes which need to be unravelled, some to do with confidence which can be built through practice, and some to do with past experiences which need to be properly dealt with. Sometimes a trading psychologist can be helpful and there is a chapter on this as well (see Chapter 16).

The top of the pyramid is the result: profits or losses. Sadly most make losses, but this is inevitable. It is one of the conundrums of trading that if everyone was perfect no one would make any money because it is a negative sum game (see Chapter 25). But this is not going to happen because people are emotional animals and many do not want to change that. They provide the fodder for the winners. This book is about how to join that select group, I hope you enjoy it.

SUMMARY

- The rules we live by in every day life do *not* work in the market environment.

- We need to construct a separate trading "personality" to succeed in the markets. This personality must learn much greater control over the emotions.

- The Trading Pyramid provides the necessary framework for this personality. Each of us will seek a different trading personality, making the most of our strengths and minimizing our weaknesses.

- The Trading Pyramid has the following levels:
  - YOU
  - Commitment
  - Discipline
  - Money management
  - Risk control
  - The three simple rules
  - System parameters
  - Your system/methodology
  - Operation
  - Profits/losses

- The structure is organic and each level interrelates with each other level.

- Trade what you see, not what you think. (Joe Ross)

Chapter 2

THE EVOLUTION OF A TRADER AND THE 55 STEPS

This chapter describes some other ways of looking at the path traders take to success.

For some years I have set out a simple process which all traders seem to encounter on the road to success. This is detailed below and thereafter I expand this in a way which I feel will be useful for those who want to tread this path.

STARTS OFF **"Greed orientated."**

Loses because:

1 Market problems
  a Not a zero sum game, a "very negative" sum game (see Chapter 25)
  b Market psychology – doing the wrong thing at the wrong time
  c The majority is always wrong
  d Market exists on chaos and confusion.
2 Own problems
  a Overtrading
  b No knowledge
  c No discipline
  c No protection against market psychology
  d Random action through uncertainty, broker's advice for example
  e Market views.

RESULT: the **"greed orientated"** trader gets a good kicking and becomes **"fear orientated."**

Loses because:

1 Market problems as above
2 Scared money never wins
3 Own problems
    a Still overtrading – derivatives
    b Fear brings on what it fears
    c Tries to cut losses too tight creating more losses
    d Still no real understanding of what it takes.

RESULT: Traders who persevere "travel through the tunnel" and becomes **"risk orientated."** This is when they start to make money because they:

1 Develop a methodology which give them an edge
2 Use an effective Money Management system
3 Develop the discipline to follow their methodology
4 Erase "harmful" personality traits.

This sets out the bare bones and you will note that there are three basic stages. As I often say it is curious that many things come in threes in the markets. Major trends can be sub-divided into three, there are three key trading rules, etc. The three key trading rules in fact equate to the three stages through which traders must pass.

The three stages

The three stages have been labeled "greed orientated," "fear orientated," and "risk orientated." However, these labels are not meant to be too literal, they are merely an attempt to approximate to the three key stages.

Greed orientated

The first stage is characterized by ignorance and the thought that the markets will provide "easy money." The actual emotion driving the new trader may not be greed, indeed it is often something else. A successful businessman or professional may be seeking a new challenge. Similar individuals may just be a little bored with their lifestyle and want something to spice it up. Others may be compulsive gamblers. One of the first problems facing a new trader is the very motivation to trade. Most people do most things emotionally. The decision as to which car to buy, which holiday to go on, etc. is usually based on emotional criteria. Just think why you own the car you do, why you married (or did not) the person you did (or did not). It is no surprise we come to the market and continue to make emotional decisions. But these will not work in the market because the market is an emotional animal itself and when the emotion is screaming *sell*, the successful trader is more likely to be buying. If we think about traders who are in the market to relieve boredom it becomes clear that the strongest impulse to trade will come when they are most bored. There is no reason why this emotional point should correspond with a good time to trade the markets. Other traders suffer from self-esteem problems, indeed I think we all do from time to time. If so, an argument with another person can again set the trader up for taking a position, to counterbalance the low self-esteem.

All these problems have to be dealt with before a trader can find success and, in my opinion, the only way in which the trader can "see" himself/herself is by using a fairly mechanical "system" so that he/she knows what he/she should be doing. In this way the trader can begin to see when his/her actions do not correspond to the system and start to question why this should be. It is through this process that we can begin to understand ourselves. I believe that this is a key requirement for trading success.

Because of these and other problems, as outlined above, novice traders lose a sufficient amount of cash to cause pain, many (most?) lose all their cash. The key point is that they become fearful as a result. At the same time they begin to realize the first secret of trading: *cut your losses*. It is this concept which marks the move to fear orientation. Indeed cutting losses can be seen as a reaction to fear.

Fear orientation

At this point stops are used, but they are generally placed too tight. The trader has realized that trading is not easy and that a lot of hard work is required. Many fall by the wayside around this point. But those who persevere do show the necessary commitment for success. But greater tests may still come and that commitment is not always enough.

Fear orientation is inevitable given the nature of the beast, i.e. the human being. The market is not terrifying, or bad, or difficult. It just is what it is, and it gets on with its own business. It is how we perceive the market and how we act that causes the problems. We must realize that we are responsible for our results, nobody else, least of all the market itself. It is only when we accept responsibility that we can start to win. If our losses are someone else's fault then we are in effect saying that we have no control. If we have no control how can we win?

> **The market is not terrifying, or bad, or difficult. It is just what it is, and it gets on with its own business.**

This stage can last a long time as we work out our various problems. Fear is not helpful in the markets because scared money never wins. We cut losers too quickly and we take profits too quickly. Our trading is characterized by nervous, over quick, action.

Risk orientation

To become risk orientated we must make progress on all fronts. Knowing ourselves, changing as need be, understanding the trading process better, adjusting our trading methodology to suit ourselves, learning to relax when trading; these are a few of the necessary requirements. Most people should immediately at least halve their trading size and that can bring immediate relief/relaxation.

Risk orientation gets its name because you need to understand risk in order to win. Trading is a risk business, when you become risk orientated your orientation is right for the market.

The key trading secret at this point is *letting profits run*. It is at this point that you may start to make consistent profits in the market. Before you reach that stage you should never trade more than the minimum size, i.e. one contract. Why pay more in tuition fees than you need?

Once risk orientated you may learn the final trading secret, *trade selectivity*. Once you have that down pat it can all become less exciting. I make money consistently but I still find myself occasionally taking too many trades. To master trade selectivity you have to become an expert in your chosen approach. The key aspect of your approach is that you

14

filter out a vast amount of market information and just focus on those factors which you need to know. It is a lot easier becoming expert in a narrow field than a wide one. The various sources of market information are so vast that it is not possible to take it all in. Let alone become an expert in it. You must decide what information you want, design your approach and then use it. Become an expert and you will find that you become intuitive, that is when you can select only the best trading positions, the low risk ones. Then it will all go the right way.

> **You must decide what information you want, design your approach and then use it.**

The 55 steps

(a personal journey to success)

(A simplified summary of the key steps taken by John Piper to get where he is today.)

1 We are intrigued by the market and start to do some preliminary reading and research.

2 We buy a book or two and perhaps some newsletters.

3 We find something we quite like and start doing some research using this particular technique.

4 We dabble a bit in the market, trading every now and then, mainly losing money, but not much, and having the occasional winner.

5 We generally forget about the losers and congratulate ourselves on our winners. Convincing ourselves that once we learn the techniques better there will be fewer of the former and more, lots more, of the latter.

6 We keep manual charts, which may become quite large physically, and maybe plot a few indicators manually (this was before computers became quite so available).

7 We spot an approach to the market we think cannot fail to win!

8 We start to trade actively.

9 The results make it clear that it is not as easy as appeared to be the case. There were a few key points we failed to fully appreciate.

10 We continue to trade. Results are fairly indifferent (to bad) but there are enough profits to keep the interest up.

11 We continue to expect great results.

12 Trading volume increases and the amount of money in the market grows.

13 We continue to read and take newsletters, but our research has only scratched the surface. We still have no real idea what we are involved with.

14 Our technique scores a major success (the '87 Crash), but our lack of trading skills means that we do not profit from it as we might.

15 The market begins to instill a little fear but we have yet to learn the first key lesson.

16 We keep trading in size. We are overtrading and clearly act as a fugitive from the law of averages. It is only a matter of time.

17 We make a big profit. It is all going well, we start to get overconfident.

18 We suffer a big loss. Psychological problems start to develop.

19 We buy a computer and start to monitor many more indicators.

20 We look at other techniques and other markets.

21 We get wiped out.

22 It becomes clear this is not at all as easy as it looks.

23 We become impossible to live with.

24 It also becomes clear that the information available (in 1987/88) is not much use to those seeking to make money from trading.

25 We determine to fill this void and look to create a newsletter telling it how it is.

26 We work with an analyst in the USA. Note how inappropriate this is for someone who wants to trade. Much better to work with a trader!

27 We continue to trade, but in a much reduced manner.

28 We start our newsletter which is an immediate success.

29 This requires a lot of research plus a lot of self analysis, but it is still not clear that trading is a psychological issue and that the externals (systems/software/computers/ brokers/advisers, etc.) are almost completely irrelevant until the internal is set up right.

30 We are plagued with fear and have no clear methodology.

31 It becomes clear that judgmental trading (without a clear methodology) is a dead end.

32 We start to look for a suitable methodology.

33 Those available on the market do not seem to be suitable and so we design our own.

34 We start to trade using a clear methodology. This is not easy but some things start to become obvious.

35 We find ourselves trading for no good reason (something that was impossible to detect before we had a clear methodology), but then realize that it is due to an argument earlier. Self esteem clearly plays a role.

36 We realize that the key element in trading is our own mentality.

Now we can start to make some real progress.

37 We improve our systems and start to make some money on a one contract basis.

38 But we are still fearful and this remains a big problem. We learnt, some time ago, the necessity of cutting losses, we cannot get to the second secret until we deal with the fear.

39 We keep trading and we continue to do OK, we start to get more confident and the fear starts to dissipate.

40 We take another big hit.

41 We feel awful and think we should perhaps give up, should perhaps have given up some years ago when it all went wrong the first time.

42 We keep trading and determine not to get overconfident again. We reinforce the stress management systems we had to learn in the early days and keep meditating (essential to trading success). We realize the importance of remaining humble and also of being an "empty vessel." If you are full of yourself there is no room to learn anything else.

43 We meet another trader who becomes a mentor. He introduces a new (to us) technique (Market Profile) which immediately "fits." This is because we now have the right attitude.

44 We build on our successes. Systems improve, results improve, and our mental attitude improves, fear becomes less of a problem.

45 We decide to see a trading coach/psychologist (Adrienne Toghraie) and have an initial meeting in Switzerland.

46 We make a big profit by letting profits run. We have managed to do what every successful trader must. Can we repeat this trick?

47 We start to move away from fear, and start to become risk orientated.

48 We realize that mental attitude is all. We see that it is vital to be relaxed, we reduce position size, again!

49 We spend a few days in the USA working in a group with our trading coach/psychologist.

50 We begin to make money with consistency.

51 We get a little overconfident, again! But this time we realize the fact and the damage is limited. But we learn, again, to remain humble.

52 We start to trade almost subconsciously some of the time. We are becoming expert.

53 We know there are still many challenges ahead but we are confident that we will deal with them.

54 Money ceases to be a problem, we truly live in a world of abundance.

55 We find that our lives improve across the board and that we are achieving in a wide range of areas.

SUMMARY

- Two different ways of looking at the same journey: the Trader's Evolution and the 55 Steps.

- Greed orientation to fear orientation to risk orientation; greed orientation leads to losses and traders become fearful. They then need to persevere and develop the skills to become risk orientated.

- The 55 Steps (every mistake in the book) depict a stylised journey which John Piper has undergone to get where he is today.

Chapter 3

THE HUMAN BRAIN

This chapter looks at two brain models which are useful when considering the way traders react to markets and why.

In 1996 I published a series of articles by Tony Plummer entitled "The Troubled Trader" (see Appendix 2). These articles were based on the concept of the "triune" brain. I also read the book *Trading Chaos* by Bill Williams which proposed another "three part" brain model. Both of these models are useful for the consideration of traders because they identify trading problems and trading solutions.

Actually Bill Williams would say that is the wrong way of looking at it. Problems do not require solutions they require transcendence. Personally I would say that these models are essential and they have allowed me to go one step further and produce the Trading Pyramid. Perhaps that is a form of transcendence.

Background reading to this chapter is *The Disciplined Trader* by Mark Douglas, the series of articles by Tony Plummer (see Appendix 2) and *Trading Chaos* by Bill Williams.

First let me explain some of the concepts from the book *Trading Chaos*. Traditional "problem" solving can create a pendulum effect. A simple example is the discipline loop which traders often go through. We acquire the discipline to follow our trading methodology, we start to make good money, we then get over-confident, we start to diverge from the discipline, we start to do badly, we are humbled, we re-learn the discipline once again, we start to do well, we again become over-confident, and so it goes. This pendulum effect is seen in the real world again and again. To succeed we have to go beyond that state, this means we have to transcend that state. Bill Williams calls this "problem solving" process a "Type One Structure," transcendence he calls a "Type

Two Structure."

He likens the comparison between these two structures to the difference between Euclidean geometry and the new "Chaos" approach to the world. I have to say I find the links to Chaos Theory in his book somewhat tenuous, but it still includes some excellent material. There is plenty about "fractals" but then they have been around for years.

Structure of the brain

Getting back to the human brain. Tony Plummer's model is in three parts: the instinctive part, the emotional part, and the thinking part – see Figure 3.1. As we evolved from the primeval swamp, or wherever it was we came from, these parts formed in turn. So the brain stem derives from our reptile heritage and is millions of years old, this provides our instinctive drives. The limbic system derives from our basic mammal heritage and involves emotional input, this too is very ancient. Of more recent development is the "neo-cortex" which involves reflective thought processes and imagination.

The problem is that trading triggers many instinctive and emotional reactions and because these reactions are so deeply buried within the functioning of our brains it is difficult for us to override them. Hence a simple activity, trading, becomes very difficult to do well. In fact this does prompt the thought that by trading we are trying to cram a square peg (ourselves) into a round hole (the trading environment). However true this may be, I would argue that by so doing we learn so much about ourselves that the process (unpleasant though it may be at times) is extremely worthwhile. Money may be the smallest of the gains we make.

I have rather sketched over the "triune" brain as discussed by Tony Plummer because this is fully covered by his article in Appendix 2.

Bill Williams' three part brain is rather different and gives rise to different considerations. He divides the brain into the three parts: the "core," the "left hemisphere" and the "right hemisphere". He doesn't particularly focus on the negative aspects of each part but more on their positive aspects. This falls in line with his Type Two Structure.

To summarize a lot of detailed material (it makes sense to read the book itself) the function of these three parts can be stated as follows. The "idiot" left hemisphere has strictly limited ability but provides the "programing" for the "core" which goes and does what needs to be done. Of the million bits of information available at any one time the "idiot" left hemisphere (which is normally in charge) can handle around 16 bits, the core can handle the lot. Hence what we do well we

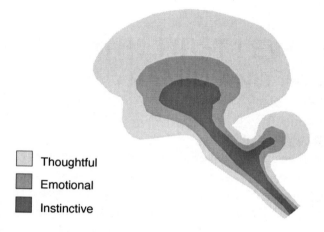

◻ Thoughtful

▨ Emotional

■ Instinctive

Fig 3.1   The triune brain

do subconsciously because the left hemisphere has trained the powerful core to do the job.

So the left hemisphere is "in charge" and here rests the ego which is filled with fear – primarily fear that it may become redundant. So it is always worrying, on the basis that if there is something to worry about it is still needed – illusory though this may be.

So what of the right hemisphere? Here we have the home of the 3 I's: Inspiration, Intuition, and Imagination (and perhaps also Insight). Some say the power of the right hemisphere is infinite, that it is a direct link to the "God Force" (call it what you will).

In Bill Williams' model, (which in many ways is a far more appealing concept – thus we may find ourselves believing it more because we believe what we want to believe) there is access to vast resource and we just have to use it by transcending our current state.

The concept of the "triune" brain fits within Bill Williams' model and subdivides, in the main, the core and the left hemisphere, although the third part of the triune brain, incorporates the right hemisphere as well. But the focus of Plummer's writing is on the problems presented by the structure of our brains and not how these problems may be transcended.

Personally I feel that the concept of the triune brain and its problems in trading are self evident. Those who have traded *know* these problems all too well. We do not need to discuss whether or not the concept is right, because we have been there.

We could perhaps say that it is only a model and as such is merely a representation of the true reality. As such perhaps it is merely a useful lie – a concept which we can use but which is not the "truth." Indeed, yes, but then so is everything, including the chair you are sitting on and the book you are holding in your hands. Everything within your mind is only a representation of the truth.

Bill William's three part brain is perhaps a little more complex, but there is plenty of evidence for its existence and its usefulness. When we learn to ride a bicycle we go through the process of trying to ride it with the idiot left hemisphere and falling off. Eventually the core becomes trained and after that it is plain sailing. Actually I managed to fall off my bicycle the other day, but we will ignore that as a red herring. We have all experienced, I expect, driving up the motorway and being unable to remember the last few miles. This is because the core has been doing it all for us. Less common is the experience of the right hemisphere taking control.

Bill Williams explains how we know which part is in control:

One of the most interesting characteristics of your intrapersonal inhabitants (the three parts of the brain) is that you can always tell in an instant which one is in command. The way the world looks to you at this moment will tell you exactly which one is in charge. If your life at this instant is a struggle, you are concerned about time and language, you dearly want to do the right thing, and/or you aren't having fun, your left hemisphere is definitely in charge. If, on the other hand, life is a series of ups and downs, you feel good physically, and you are having a good time, you are operating from your core. If life is absolutely a bowl of cherries and everything in the world seems to be geared to giving you exactly what you want, you are in the right hemisphere.

An illustration of how these three parts interact in the trading environment described in *Trading Chaos* is reproduced in Figure 3.2. If you trade with *only* the right hemisphere you will have bad management, so you will lose. If you trade with only the core you will be reckless, or with only the left hemisphere you will be scared. If you trade without the left hemisphere you don't have the experience, without the core you don't have confidence, and without the right hemisphere you don't have intu-

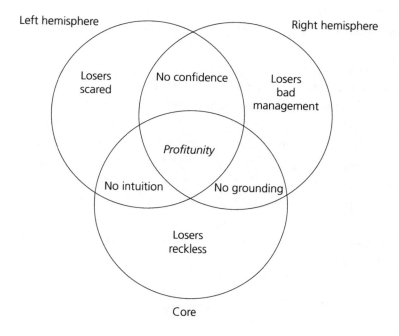

Fig 3.2   Bill Williams' brain model

Source: Williams, B (1995) *Trading Chaos*, © John Wiley & Sons, Inc. Reprinted with permission.

ition. It is when all three parts are working in harmony you get what Bill Williams calls "profitunity."

Trading Chaos

The layout of *Trading Chaos* is designed to get you there. The book offers five stages, each including different goals, and different tools to help you attain those goals. The five stages are: novice, advanced beginner, competent, proficient and expert. The goals are respectively; to minimize losses, to make money consistently on a one-contract basis, to maximize your profits, to trade your own belief systems, and to trade your states of mind. Each stage offers better tools to achieve these objectives. In this context tools refers to analysis techniques plus your own inherent abilities.

The book doesn't tell you how to tap the vast potential of your necktop computer but then this has been the goal of all mystics and spiritual gurus through the ages and is perhaps too much to expect. But if you want to see the Holy Grail, look in a mirror!

I have written this chapter because I believe the more we understand about ourselves the easier it will be to find success in the markets. The chapter may seem incomplete but it will be many decades, or even centuries, before we, as human beings, have a full understanding of ourselves, if indeed we ever do. So do not expect precise answers; and they are probably not even desirable. What you need are subtle signposts to steer you in the right direction (possibly such signposts should be aimed at parts of the brain other than the left hemisphere), I hope this one helps.

SUMMARY

- I discuss two models of the human brain.

- The triune brain (see Appendix 2) offers a guide to why we often make a mess of trading.

- The Bill Williams' brain model offers a guide to how we might want our brains to function to optimize performance.

- The triune brain consists of three parts, the Emotional, the Instinctive and the Thoughtful. All three have a vital part to play in our lives but the first two can be very destructive when trading the markets.

- The Bill Williams' model is more physically based, consisting, again, of three parts. In this case the left hemisphere, the right hemisphere and the core. The left hemisphere brings management and learning to the table, the core operational ability, and the right hemisphere, intuition, inspiration and imagination. When all three parts are working in harmony we have "Profitunity," as Bill William puts it.

Chapter 4

YOU – THE FIRST LEVEL OF THE PYRAMID AND WHY

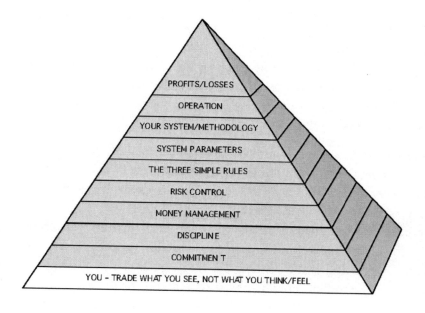

PROFITS/LOSSES

OPERATION

YOUR SYSTEM/METHODOLOGY

SYSTEM PARAMETERS

THE THREE SIMPLE RULES

RISK CONTROL

MONEY MANAGEMENT

DISCIPLINE

COMMITMENT

YOU – TRADE WHAT YOU SEE, NOT WHAT YOU THINK/FEEL

We lie loudest when we lie to ourselves.

Eric Hoffer

There are many fundamental misconceptions about markets and trading. I have a natural talent for analysis. I wish I had more of a natural talent for trading, but I do not. I have got where I have despite my abilities, not because of them. But my analysis has helped a lot, because I now understand markets and how to make money out of them. I now make consistent profits and as each year goes by those profits get bigger.

This book is not verbose, it cuts to the essentials. I might summarize these essentials as follows:

1 You may think that the market exists somewhere out there. **Wrong**. How you think of the market is unique and exists only in your head. To win you have to ensure that your version of the market is "useful" and then make use of it.

2 You may think you see your version of the market clearly. **Wrong**. What you see is shrouded within an emotional whirlwind. The whirlwind may get a lot faster when you have a trading position in place.

> *To win you have to ensure that your version of the market is "useful" and then make use of it.*

3 You may think that trading is an easy function involving buying low and selling high. **Wrong**. In fact trading is not difficult, although nor is it easy, but the emotional problems we bring with us to the market mean that few win.

These three statements summarize what you are getting into. In normal walks of life these sort of things either do not happen or we soon learn to stay away. The market is different. It does not do the same things all the time. So one day a particular tactic will work, the next day it won't. Compare this with a normal everyday function like walking down the street. If you walk into a lamp post, you soon learn that you need to walk round them. But in the market-place, the lamp posts keeps moving as you approach them, you can never be sure that you can get round them.

But what you can do is develop the mental discipline so that even when you do bump into them it's OK.

This section is entitled "YOU." This is because you are the essential element behind the way you trade. If you refer to the diagram of the Trading Pyramid at the beginning of this chapter you will see that **you** form the base of the pyramid. This is because you have to develop a style of trading which suits **you**. In no other way is it going to work.

The trading experience

If you peruse any bookshop with a few books on trading you will soon find that there are masses of people out there seeking to grab some of your hard earned cash so that they can tell you about how **they** trade the markets, although in many cases these authors do not actually trade themselves, but that is another matter. Now it may be that one of these many books is right for you, but which one? Not an easy question to answer. Apart from the analysis technique you should use, you also have to learn trading skills, which ultimately are about 95 per cent of this game. This takes time. Do not expect to be an instant success at trading, you have to learn this business as you do any other. Whilst you do so you have a simple task and this is the first **secret** of trading. Like all great secrets it is well known, because that is the best way to keep something a secret, make everyone think it is not a secret at all. But this is where most novice traders fall down, this is where they knock themselves out of the game. I am not going to repeat this secret now because to do so would be to belittle its importance. This secret, plus the other two are revealed

> *In the trading environment there is no absolute truth.*

throughout this book. When you hear the secrets you will already "know" them but maybe this time they will have sufficient impact to make a difference. That is all I ask, that what I say helps to make a difference, to improve your trading performance.

To introduce the trading experience we must look inside ourselves. This is where it all takes place. There are a few simple rules but before saying what they are I think it is important to stress three points:

1 In the trading environment there is no absolute truth. We never know what is the "right" thing to do in any one situation and what is "right" for one trader is wrong for another. We therefore have to formulate "useful beliefs" which work for us. This is akin to how scientists work when dealing with quantum mechanics. The building block of all matter, according to current theories (or useful beliefs), is a quark. But this is found to have no mass. How can the building block have no mass? Another word for a useful belief is a useful lie. Anything which is not the truth, the whole truth, and nothing but the truth, can be said to be a lie, although this definition is not widely accepted.

2 Given this fact nothing I say is cast in stone, it is important you discover your own "useful lies" that will form the basis of your trading philosophy.

3 In similar vein it is your personality which should guide you in your search for the right approach. Do not be guided by advertising copy, as many are. Ask the question "What is right for me?" and then go out and find it.

So what are the few simple rules? In my opinion they are as follows:

1 Always limit your losses.
2 Try to ensure that your average gain is at least 2.5 times your average loss.
3 Endeavour to find an approach which gives you an edge.
4 Make sure you are comfortable with your trading approach. This involves self discovery, something many shy away from. But peal away the outer layers and what is inside is often very fine indeed. The outward layers can be a bit yukky.
5 Learn to let profits run.
6 Learn to trade selectively.
7 Learn to control your own self sabotage.

SUMMARY

- YOU - the first level of the Trading Pyramid because the whole pyramid has to be based on your personality.

- How we each see the market is unique and we need to ensure that our perception is "useful."

- The key trading "secrets" are well known.

- In the trading environment there is no "absolute" truth.

- Nothing in this book is "cast in stone" and you must find your own road to success.

- Don't be led by advertising copy, decide what you need and then go and get it.

- There are seven simple rules to success.

Chapter 5

COMMITMENT

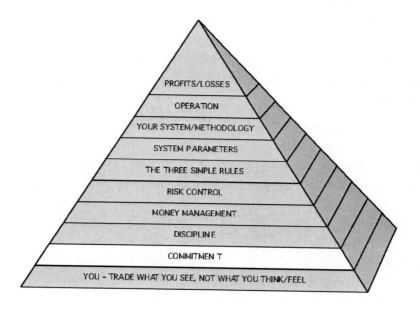

To many traders the market is a generator of random sequences. In many cases it will drive you round the bend. Commitment is a very necessary quality if you are going to be a winner.

The nature of the market

Whether the market is such a generator depends on your perception of the market. For example if you choose to trade the market on the basis of a precise algorithm, i.e. a precise formula such as used by stochastics, moving averages, etc., then you are dependent on exactly what the market throws at you. In this sense it is such a generator. If, however, you choose to look at something which has "meaning" then the market will not be solely such a generator. However, most of the chart patterns, etc. that are used are fairly meaningless. This is illustrated by two facts:

1 For something to have meaning it has to be right more than half the time. Strictly, the variance from the 50/50 criterion has to have statistical relevance.

2 Very often, no sooner do we see a "pattern" than it aborts. It was never really there in the first place. It just so happens that the market, in its function as a generator of random sequences, is going to throw out all types of "pattern" but that does not mean that they have any meaning.

I became interested in markets via the Elliott Wave Theory (EWT). This is a good example of what I consider fairly meaningless. The theory is general enough that there are going to be lots of random sequences meeting its criterion. Some of them work, some of them don't. I doubt the ratio is much away from 50 per cent. But I find I am now indoctrinated in EWT, see Appendix 5, so I have learnt to live with it. I now ensure that I only take signals which have something meaningful attached to them – for example, Minus Development from Market Profile (see Chapter 18).

So what does have meaning? In my view the only fact that can be stated about markets is as follows:

Markets move from extreme to extreme across all time frames.

Markets are a manifestation of human psychology. They are driven by fear and greed. Peaks are driven by greed, troughs by fear. This is obvious in the very long-term extremes. Fear is often illustrated, literally, with blood in the street. Greed is so endemic nobody recognizes it for what it is. But stand aside and it becomes obvious. Not so obvious in the shorter term moves, but still there. At the extremes the key point is that price is stretched unrealistically. Why is this? Because traders and/or investors are paying too much, selling too cheaply, because it is an *emotional* decision. To win you must put yourself outside that emotion.

Extremes are detectable and I have built an array of tactics for spotting them – see Section 2.

Market Profile

There is something else we can use, and this is Market Profile developed by Peter Steidlmayer. The concept is simple and built around the bell curve. A bell curve takes chaos and substitutes order. Market Profile is another way of displaying market action. Other ways are:

1 A quote screen.
2 A bar chart.
3 A tick chart.
4 A Point and Figure chart.
5 Candlesticks.
6 All the various indicators.

All of the above (and others, as this is not meant to be exhaustive) display the same thing in a different way. In all cases you lose some information but other information is highlighted. To an extent this is your first decision point. What is the most useful way for you to look at market action? The answer to this critically important question depends on how you are going to

> **If it is not obvious why something should work, it probably doesn't!**

trade and what you therefore need to see to do so. Don't put the cart before the horse. Decide what you want and then go and get it. Do not get something because someone sells it to you and then adapt yourself to that, it is the wrong way round. Incidentally, modern software is such that you can often have a number of the above all on the same screen layout. My software will give me all of the above on one layout and it is not expensive. But I don't use them all because I see no need to.

Market Profile has a number of key concepts. To my mind the most important is Minus Development (MD). MD is merely a technique which shows determined buying or selling. It is fairly obvious, as are most useful techniques. Indeed I would say that if it is not obvious why something should work, it probably doesn't! MD comes in various shapes and sizes, but I consider the most important to be spike highs or lows. In fact most of my own trading is concerned with just these. The key concept is that MD shows where price is swiftly rejected. You want your stop to be beyond such a point, that way it is relatively secure. If you want total security, you had better get out of the market and call in Securicor. Gaps are also a form of MD but I do not like gaps so much because a market will try to close any gaps. There is a simple reason for this: the aim of any market is to maximize trade. You can prove this by looking at who runs the market and how they get paid. In the case of a futures market it is organized and run by the Exchange itself (LIFFE in the case of FTSE, CME in the case of the S&P), the brokers and the market makers. All of

The aim of any market is to maximize trade.

these make more money the more trading there is, so that is the aim of their market. In order to maximize trade a market must trade at all levels because there will be buyers and sellers at each of those levels. Or there may be, so the market has to check and see – if it is efficient. So gaps get closed, at least on markets that are actively traded, like the FTSE futures. Not so much on the FTSE cash, because this is just an index, it is not actually traded. In fact since the introduction of the appalling SETS system the FTSE cash no longer leaves gaps.

SUMMARY

- The market can be seen as a generator of random sequences, if you follow a precise trading system, that is exactly what it is.

- You have got to have commitment to succeed. The road to success has many pitfalls and those who lack commitment will be easily dissuaded.

- Markets move from extreme to extreme across all time frames. This is the only absolute truth we have about markets.

- Different ways of looking at market action all serve to highlight some information; whilst minimizing or eliminating other elements.

- Market Profile and Minus Development are ways of looking at the market which have some meaning and may, therefore, prove more useful than other techniques.

- The market is designed to generate trade and maximize it. This is a fundamental fact it is always well to remember.

Chapter 6

DISCIPLINE

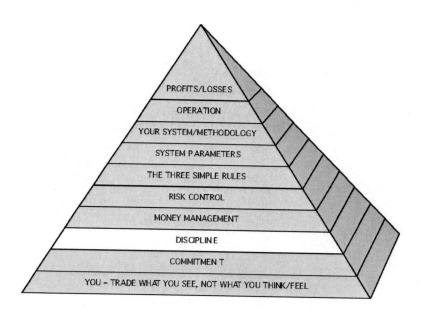

The next level of the pyramid is discipline. It is said, and it is true, that without discipline you will be unable to make any progress. The reason is simple and comes in a number of guises. First, without discipline you will be unable to follow your own methodology, you will, in effect, have no methodology. Thus you will be doomed to trade emotionally, and that is not a winning approach. Second, you will not have the self discipline to overcome your own emotions and instincts. So in some ways these two factors overlap, but the second is far more pervasive than simply in operating your methodology.

The big question here is whether you can develop the discipline if you do not have it naturally. I believe that the answer is "yes, you can," but you must have the necessary commitment to do so.

Clearly discipline can be developed, and you only need to look at an army training program for confirmation of this fact. But it is one thing to have a vast and experienced organization bearing down on you and prepared to do whatever it takes to make its point, quite another to do it yourself in the comfort of your own home, with all the distractions that normally involves. Clearly self discipline is going to be a requirement even to start the process.

However, the market itself is going to be helpful, although not as helpful as it might be. Ultimately undisciplined behavior is going to be punished by the market, either by direct losses or by the loss of profits which would otherwise have been available. So private traders who persevere do have external stimuli that help the process. But the market does not help as much as it might because of the principle of random reinforcement. I will mention this again. It is the market's tendency to reward bad behavior from time to time. What works one day may not work the next and this applies to the "best" trading practice. Similarly bad habits do bring rewards from time to time. This crucial fact is one of the reasons that it takes so long to learn how to trade.

Discipline and the Trading Pyramid

So, let us look at discipline within the context of the Trading Pyramid. We have already discussed how the various levels of the pyramid interact. Now I want to concentrate on how this interaction relates to discipline. There is a great deal of difference

> **If you find an approach that suits you, it will be much easier to follow.**

between applying discipline to doing something you like, as opposed to something you don't like. For example if you like playing a particular sport, say tennis, then you may find it very easy to be disciplined when taking shots, keeping score, following court etiquette, and the rest. No problem, because you would enjoy the whole thing. But say you had to go fishing and you couldn't stand it. Would you have the same discipline with baiting the hook, casting the line, sitting patiently waiting for a bite, etc.? No, you wouldn't. You would probably be slapdash and sloppy, you would probably fidget, when you need to be still. It is the same with trading. If you find an approach that suits you, it will be much easier to follow. You will avoid trying to squeeze a square peg (yourself) into a round hole (your market approach). This applies to every level of the pyramid. Your Money Management (MM) system is designed to keep you safe so that you can relax. Much easier to apply discipline in such an environment. Risk Control has a similar function. It is all about making you comfortable and developing the skills to keep your losses under control. Again this makes the trader's situation a lot more comfortable. Moving up to the next level we come to the three simple rules. The logic of these rules is unassailable. However, we have to learn how to use them and this takes time, especially learning to let profits run. After all the skills needed to cut losses are almost exactly the opposite of those required to let profits run. The first requires careful monitoring and quick action (maybe using a stop in the market to do it for you) whereas the latter requires a more relaxed approach to avoid getting out. So one is actively looking to get out, the other is passively not looking to get out. Once you have learnt actively to look to get out, how do you then totally adjust your view to achieve the other? It takes time.

It is easy to see how we can be a lot more relaxed, and therefore more disciplined once we have learnt how to operate these rules. Some readers may feel that linking the words "relaxed" and "disciplined" is something of an oxymoron, or two incompatible concepts. I disagree. In my view relaxation is the essence of "easy" discipline. You do not need to be tense and standing to attention to be disciplined. You just need to be able to do certain things in a certain way. The easier these things are, because you choose what they are, the more experience you have in doing them, clearly the easier they will be to do.

System parameters

This brings us to your system parameters. It is going to take time to discover these. This is not because there is any particular magic about the parameters themselves, but because you need to know yourself well before you will be able to judge what is going to suit you. There is a feedback loop involved in this process. Once you start to use a more precise methodology that feedback loop can start. Until that point most traders are just spinning their wheels. Once you start to use a methodology you begin to learn a lot about yourself. This is because you start to see when you have difficulties with the methodology. You are forced to stop and ask yourself. "Why did I not take that trade?" and, perhaps more importantly, "Why did I take this trade which has nothing to do with my methodology?" Often you find that you

> **Why did I take this trade which has nothing to do with my methodology?**

have certain preconceptions which are not useful, that you have impulses to trade that have nothing to do with making money, but have everything to do with various emotions you have not yet learnt to control. At least that was my experience.

It is the feedback from these things you learn about yourself that allows you to modify your methodology. This process, which takes you round the loop many times, eventually allows you to discover something that is truly useful to **you**. It will not necessarily be useful to anyone else. This is why I am always distrustful of those who claim to have market "secrets" they will not disclose. To my mind this shows a misunderstanding of the entire process, although I can see why someone would not want to disclose their entire methodology. The more people who trade "your way" the less likely that way is to be effective. But even this is debatable as any trader who looks at another's methodology is liable to alter it and trade it in their own way. However there is no point in taking any chances in this respect, why take the risk?

SUMMARY

- Discipline is necessary because without it you will not be able to follow your methodology, or to control your emotions and instincts.

- Developing discipline is a process rather like exercising muscles, but is helped by developing an approach that suits us.

- Random reinforcement is the way in which the market often rewards "bad" behaviour and punishes "good behaviour". Rats go mad when treated like this.

- Inter-reactions between discipline and other levels of the Pyramid show the importance of developing all levels of the Pyramid in line with our personalities.

Chapter 7

MONEY MANAGEMENT

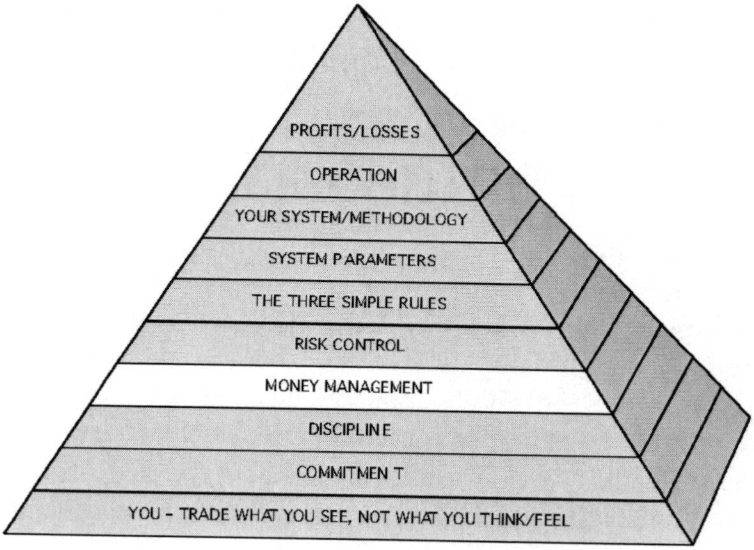
PROFITS/LOSSES
OPERATION
YOUR SYSTEM/METHODOLOGY
SYSTEM PARAMETERS
THE THREE SIMPLE RULES
RISK CONTROL
MONEY MANAGEMENT
DISCIPLINE
COMMITMENT
YOU - TRADE WHAT YOU SEE, NOT WHAT YOU THINK/FEEL

I often say in my newsletter (*TTT*) that Money Management (MM) is far more important than analysis. But I have never given a practical example of how this should work. This chapter is designed to remedy this omission.

It is easy to demonstrate that MM is far more important than analysis. A total lack of MM would mean risking everything on any one trade. You might have the best analysis system in the world and get 99 straight trades right but that 100th trade would wipe you out. On the other hand you might have the worst analysis system in the world. If so a proper MM system will quickly reveal this fact which at the same time minimizing the risk to your capital. So if you get 10 straight trades wrong you still only lose 10 per cent of your capital! It is therefore immediately clear which is the more important. MM is what makes the analysis/system work not the other way around.

The conclusion from this is that it is not entry which is that important – it is exit. This is clearly so, because exit determines your overall risk, your overall profit and your overall control. Now this is quite a controversial statement. If entry is not so important why do all traders spend so much time on it. The answer is because they are misguided. Clearly entry is also important, but not as important as the other factors in trading, in particular MM and Risk Control (RC). To put this in a nutshell: your entry cannot wipe you out – but the way you exit can. Your entry does not make you a profit – the way you exit can.

> **It is not entry which is that important – it is exit.**

Using Money Management

So how do you use MM practically? For this I will use an illustration concerning one of my trading services. This sets out the MM rules behind this. This is universally applicable to any trading approach not merely to this system. The essential factor behind any winning approach is that it gives you an "edge." Without an edge it is impossible to win – if anybody doubts this please e-mail me to discuss it. I consider that my methodology gives me an edge of around 60–70 per cent. This has to be related to a random process which could be gauged at 50 per cent. The figure of 50 per cent is not totally accurate as it ignores the costs of trading, but we will over discount for this factor by assuming that my approach will yield a success rate of 55 per cent. It now comes to apply an MM system to this. Let us assume that a trader has £10,000 he is prepared to lose. As a general rule a 20 per cent loss is considered the time to get out – so we are assuming that the trader has capital of £50,000 of which he is prepared to lose £10,000. With £10,000 our MM rule is that we are not prepared to lose more than 10 per cent per trade (i.e. £1000) and this equates to 100 points on a single FTSE futures contract, or 50 points on two contracts. If we adopt this approach it means we would have to suffer 10 trades in a row to be wiped out of the market – i.e. we would lose our £10,000 (20 per cent of our total trading capital of £50,000). So we then take our expected success rate of 55 per cent and see what the odds are of making 10 successive losing trades. The odds on this are 45 per cent (the failure rate being 100 per cent less 55 per cent) to the power of 10. This comes down to 0.035 per cent – i.e. 3.5 times out of 10 000 trades. The 45 per cent failure rate also shows us that we have a 1 in 10 chance of making three losses in a row, a four out of 100 chance of four losses in a row, and a 2 out of 100 chance

> *It is my view that any one trade should not incur risk of more than 2 per cent.*

of five losses in a row. These odds make sense and we can see how this approach can be monitored to ensure that the original assumptions are correct. If so, it is also easy to go further and to develop confidence in the approach. Now to some of you a 100 point stop may seem a little high, but there are ways to mitigate this exposure and at less risk. You will also note how applying 10 per cent to one fifth of the capital equates to 2 per cent of all of the capital. It is my view that any one trade should not incur risk of more than 2 per cent.

Position size

The above sets out one way of approaching Money Management. I believe that this is an eminently practical way of approaching this extremely important area of trading. Now I want to say a few words about position size. Let us assume that you have just devised a new system and that your testing of this system has led you to believe that it is excellent. Let us also say that you have £100 000 of trading capital and that you can hardly wait for those megabucks of profit you are going to make – so off you go, at least 10 contracts right from the start. Right? No, **wrong!** Paper trading is useful, testing is useful, but when you start to play for real the game changes, if only because you start to hit emotional/psychological problems you never even dreamt existed. These problems can be overcome but when you enter a new arena (i.e. actually trading your new system/approach) then you must minimize your risk – indeed good traders minimize risk at all times. So you don't trade 10 contracts, you trade just one. And you keep trading just one until your *actual results* confirm that you should increase position size. At that point the area of risk (new territory) has become more quantified and you can move ahead without that being such a worry. It would then make sense to increase position size in appropriate steps. What you stand to gain from this approach is obvious. If your system had some flaws then you do not lose all your capital and you also develop some discipline along the way. What do you stand to lose? Just a little time. If all goes according to plan you may well be trading at the size you originally wanted to just a few months later – and in real terms that is nothing. What I find frustrating is that I can explain this to consultancy clients until I am blue in the face but then they often ignore the advice, go off over-trading, survive for a while, maybe even make some money, then that trade with their number comes along and its "adios amigo!"

Monitoring position

Another area where we can reduce risk is in careful monitoring of a position in the early stages. Sometimes when looking at a bar chart it is obvious where the market diverged from the expected path. Such divergence is a warning sign and often a very strong one. Indeed one factor I have noticed is that once a market diverges from a pattern that often a very strong move comes in the other way. The logic of this is fairly clear in that there will be plenty of traders, following the original signal, who will be caught out by just such a move. To an extent the need for careful monitoring will depend on your entry methodology and the logic/philosophy behind it. If you are looking for entries which ought to catch "unacceptable" prices then you would want such prices to be swiftly rejected by the market. The lack of such rejection might be a reason to exit a position. After all you are looking for the best opportunities and one which does not show such rejection may well not make that grade. Such things have to be related to each individual's trading style and time frame. But this is where a real time price service can pay for itself. Signal, Tenfore, or Market Eye, for example, all cost considerably less than £300 per month and that is only 30 points on a FTSE futures contract. Of course then you need to be around to watch the screen, but the danger area is at the beginning of the trade. That is when you are most vulnerable, so it is really a question of monitoring the progress early on; once the trade has gone the right way traders can relax a little.

Stops can be a central feature of an MM system. There are various ways in which stops can be utilized and these will be covered in Chapter 15. That concludes our brief resume of some of the more important points of MM, a subject of many books. But it should serve to prompt a few thoughts about how you might be able to improve your approach to the market.

SUMMARY

- Good Money Management is the key to success. Without it even the best trading system would wipe you out.

- A good MM approach means adopting a low risk approach to each trade. If you don't do that it is a racing certainty that you will be wiped out.

- Starting with a new system you must use just one contract until your results, i.e. profits, prove that it works for real.

- Early and careful monitoring of a new position can minimize risk even more, but don't be suckered out prematurely.

Chapter 8

RISK CONTROL

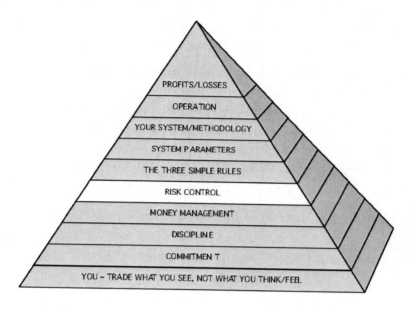

The traders who win are those who minimize risk. This is another key chapter and its importance is such that readers should read it carefully and ensure they understand its contents. Those who do not minimize risk inevitably pay the price and get wiped out.

It is for this reason that you often see strong moves after a news item is out of the way, often a news item suggesting a strong move in the opposite direction. The big traders, who got that way by minimizing risk in the first place, wait until the risk is at its lowest, when the news is out of the way.

Risk Control includes the following:

1 Not trading in too big a size, thus reducing the risk of a wipe out. Actually you should eliminate the risk of a wipe out .

2 Not holding overnight unless you have a profit buffer in place.

However this does not apply to particular methodologies seeking to take advantage of certain factors which may apply to holding overnight.

3 Not holding over the weekend, subject to the same caveats as "2" above.

4 Taking appropriate action prior to major new items. This means not normally opening positions, maybe reducing position size if already positioned – although it does depend on your trading objectives.

But in markets there are two types of risk and we need to look at both. First there is the risk of loss inherent in the market itself. Second there is the risk of loss inherent in the vehicle we are trading. I deal with this in more detail later on (see Chapter 10), but simply put, the risk of making a losing trade when buying an option is far higher than when writing an option. But you can lose a lot more writing options, than you can buying them. This neatly demonstrates the two types of risk and, as traders, we need to understand how this works.

Risk inherent in the vehicle

First we will look at the risk inherent in the vehicle. This is really part of knowing your vehicles well and, as such, is part of the initial learning curve. If we take the example of buying a call option for 25 points. Our maximum loss is 25 points, we simply cannot lose more than that. So whatever happens we are safe, as long as that 25 points fits within our Money Management system. IBM, ICI, Microsoft and JP Morgan could all go bust and it would not make any difference. This is a very different situation to that in place if we had decided to go long either by writing put options, or by buying futures. In both those cases we would have lost point for point with the index futures (or whatever it was we were trading). Clearly a very different kettle of fish!

IBM, ICI, Microsoft and JP Morgan could all go bust and it would not make any difference.

This gives rise to a useful point. As traders we want to keep as many options open as possible (I don't mean market options in this context).

In certain situations one trading vehicle may offer a better deal. For example a cheap option may make sense if we want to trade ahead of a news item. A pair of cheap options (i.e. a put and a call) may make sense if we expect a big move but do not know in which direction – I adopted this strategy the Friday before the 1987 Crash on the OEX Options. A deep-in-the-money option may make more sense than trading the futures on occasion. This is because first, it may cheaper, and second, it might put on time value as the intrinsic value reduced. So it might give you more on the upside, at a lower risk on the downside. All of these can be very useful in trading markets and it is critically important that a trader is fully aware of the risk profile of the vehicle traded. This is simply because this impacts on the risk profile offered by the market itself.

Risk inherent in the market

This brings us back to the risk inherent in the market itself. My experience is that when we start to trade, we trade in blissful ignorance of this risk – what some would call a fool's paradise. We then get a good kicking and become fearful. Yes, we are back to the Traders' Evolution as set out in Chapter 2. Finally we become "Risk Orientated." That is our goal. So risk goes to the heart of the trading experience. It is learning to live with risk that defines the trading experience. It is our stock in trade, even more than money. Money is the result once we learn to control risk. To an extent this whole book is about risk control. That is what Money Management does, that is what the three simple rules do, that is what our entire trading system does, and discipline allows us to control risk by using these other tools correctly. However, this section is about avoiding the more obviously high levels of risk which the market regularly encounters, mainly in the form of expected news items.

Other forms of risk

But there are also many other unexpected forms of risk. Even when a news item is expected its content can come as a big surprise. In my experience most market shocks come in whilst the market is open, but that is not always the case. Often markets do see sharp action into the open as they are forced to digest some event that has occurred whilst they have been closed. The trend towards 24-hour markets, evidenced by Globex, can be useful in this respect but, as traders, we cannot be awake 24 hours a day; we have to sleep. Also these markets are not ideal; they tend to be traded rather thinly and thus exaggerate any move that comes their way. Often the level of the S&P futures on Globex is not representative of what the official

it is rare that the news really has any lasting effect.

S&P futures do when they open for real. But even with Globex, once the news is out you are not going to get the right price. But that is not the point. I see no reason to trade off news items, it is rare that the news really has any effect. At least any lasting effect. Many will recoil from this statement in disbelief. But the fact is that "markets move from extreme to extreme across all time frames," good or bad news becomes irrelevant within that context. The market will just keep rolling until it has reached the next extreme. What marks the major extremes are two key, but linked factors. First is the extreme psychology, "you must own stocks" (which we have in the late 1990s) as opposed to the converse philosophy, "stocks are far too risky" (which was all pervasive in the mid-1970s). These extreme statements define the psychology and define the peaks and troughs. The one being seen now drags everyone into the market. When everyone is in, there is no one left to buy and so the market will go down. It is very difficult to time such extremes, but there is no doubt that a large fall is coming, it may have started. Similarly the statement, "stocks are far too risky" defines an extreme low, no one wanted to own stocks, hence it could only go up.

In this context the market is very much like a mechanical device. Having gone one way and reached that extreme, it has no choice but to go the other way.

However, when trading derivatives we cannot key into these very large moves and have to have regard to the shorter term action. Indeed it can be a mistake to ignore any extreme, however small the time frame, because everything has to start somewhere.

To get back to news items. For my own trading purposes I use them to enter the way I wanted to in the first place. What I like to see is when the market reacts positively to "bad" news or negatively to "good" news. Not that I really believe in such classifications. There is no such thing as good or bad news, it all depends on your perceptions and what comes next. Often very good events follow "bad" news, and very bad things happen as a result of "good" news (see Chapter 25).

So traders should use the news to suit themselves. Don't view it as a negative, merely adjust position size (maybe to nil) ahead of the news and then use the prices generated subsequently to your advantage.

I believe there is less risk holding overnight or over a weekend than there is holding into a news item. But the longer the time when the market is closed, the more that can happen, so this also must be considered.

SUMMARY

- You must minimize risk if you are going to win.

- There are two types of risk in the market:
  1 There is the risk inherent in your trading vehicles.
  2 There is the risk inherent in the market itself.

- The market mechanism drives price from one extreme to the other. Once an extreme is reached price can only go one way.

- Good news and bad news represent risk, but the market can provide excellent indications that an extreme may have been seen.

Chapter 9

THE THREE SIMPLE RULES (OR TRADING SECRETS)
3 2 3

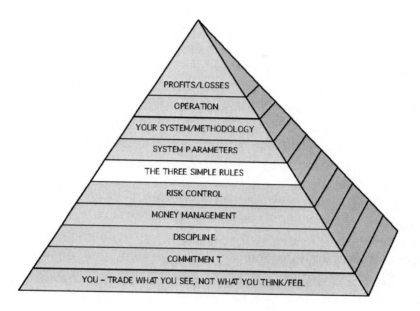

We discussed secrets in Chapter 5. The best place to hide a secret is where everyone can see it. Then they don't think it is a secret. This is true of these secrets. I have subtitled this 3 2 3 because the number 3 keeps cropping up.

First it cropped up in both of our brain models. Tony Plummer's triune brain composed of three parts: the instinctive, the emotive, and the thinking parts. The model from *Trading Chaos* also consisted of three, but different parts: the left hemisphere, the core, and the right hemisphere. As it happens these last three are linked in with the three trading "secrets." Secrets you all know well, but perhaps you do not realize their importance. I know I did not when I started.

The left hemisphere thinks it is clever, it has "added" **ego**, that likes to show off. It doesn't like to get it wrong. It finds taking losses difficult because that means admitting it is wrong. You must train it differently, or at least train the core which can then take on this difficult task.

The trading secrets

Secret 1: Cut your losses

The first function that the new trader must accomplish is to learn the business (instruct the core). Whilst doing so the key is to minimize your tuition fees, so cut those losses, because they are your tuition fees. The money spent on software, newsletters, books, seminars etc. is often trivial in comparison.

As we learn the business we find that we tend to churn away without getting very far. We learn to cut losses, but find that we make plenty of good trades but not only are we cutting losses, we are also cutting our profits. No surprise there. The **ego**, desperate for anything positive, takes any profit it sees. But this is also no good because if you are going to make money you have got to take those big profits. To do so you need:

Secret 2: Run your profits

OK, now you are starting to make progress. You should be making consistent profits on a one contract basis. But you have not cracked it yet. You have not competed all of the 55 steps (see Chapter 2), nor are you fully through the Trader's Evolution (again see Chapter 2). But you have your core on your side and your right hemisphere is starting to get involved. Now you can start to implement the final secret:

Secret 3: Trade selectivity

You have got to learn how to pick only the best opportunities. This takes time. You have got to find the right trading approach for yourself. You have got to narrow your focus on the market. There is far too much information out there to absorb, even for your right hemisphere. So decide on your methodology, concentrate on what you need, and become an expert in its application. When you do this you will know which are the best opportunities and which are not. At the same time you will need to develop the mental discipline and patience to wait for just those opportunities.

Actually I will give you an added bonus:

Secret 4: Trade with the trend

That way you will have many more winners.

Following the rules

Now let's look at the practical problems in following these three "simple" rules. You would think that cutting losses would be simple enough. It is hardly a difficult concept after all. But it does bring a lot of additional baggage with it. It certainly makes the whole trading approach a lot more complex. But the alternative is to be wiped out – at least for the majority.

We will first look at the basic philosophy. If you risk too big a percentage of your capital on any one trade, then you are liable to be wiped out. So you must choose an entry mechanism which allows low risk entries, meaning the risk is a low percentage of your capital.

Using stops

Having got to that point novice traders are forced to use market stops because they rarely have the skill to use one of the many alternatives. But immediately trading becomes more complex, because you keep on getting stopped out! Unfortunately that is just one of the things traders have to get used to. Particularly so when the market triggers your stop and then goes off in the direction you intended. That will happen a lot as well!

But I think the philosophy is obvious and I have yet to hear a good argument for not using stops in derivative markets, although I accept that some traders work better without them. It is different with stocks, where the gearing is not in place, and it can be different when trading with fundamentals. But beginners do not have the pockets or the experience to do this.

Now to the practical problems of using stops. These come in a whole range of shapes and forms. Let's start with the most simple human urge, as expressed in everyday life. When we see something we want, we grab it; when we see something we dislike, we often drive it from our minds – let's forget about it, it will probably go away. In the real world this may not hurt too much, but in the markets, losses that are treated this way tend to get bigger. It is a basic human urge to ignore bad things, thus we are pre-programed not to take losses, but we are also pre-programed to take profits as soon as we see them. Think about your life so far and the way you live it. How easy do you think it would be to change some of your basic behavioral characteristics? Pretty tough? Well that is what you have to do to follow the first two simple rules.

Losses

> *Before starting to trade make sure you are happy being wrong a lot of the time – it might save you a fortune.*

Then there is the dear old ego. Guess what? Most of us do not like being wrong. Most of us associate losing money with being wrong. Guess what? We would rather avoid taking a loss, which will then probably get worse, than admit we might be wrong. Some traders talk about how much a novice trader is prepared to pay before admitting he is wrong. What is your price, £1000, £2000, £5000, or are you in the £100 000 category along with some others I know? Before starting to trade make sure you are happy being wrong a lot of the time – it might save you a fortune.

But a lot of traders I know agree with all this and still big losses somehow creep up on them. They have on me in the past. Normally this occurs when we change something about our trading. Perhaps we increase position size, perhaps we start trading a new market, perhaps we hold overnight for a change. Whatever it might be it is often a stumbling block. Something is a little different and until you are experienced and well practiced, the smallest thing can get in the way between you and properly operating your stop policy. So be on your guard.

Most traders learn their lessons the hard way and learning to cut losses is usually the hardest of all because it is the most painful. Most traders admit to that one trade that went horribly wrong, and I suspect those that don't admit it also experienced it. They just prefer to hide it away, maybe even from themselves. Far better to be open, especially with yourself.

The sequence of events is that we take a trade and we do not put a stop in the market. Or if we do put a stop in place we do not do it GTC (good till cancelled) and it would have got hit the next day. Whatever, the trade goes against us and we suddenly find that the loss is bigger than we planned. That is the first problem area. We have, in effect, rehearsed taking a loss of x, but 2x was not envisioned. We go through stages of fear, denial, hope, and the rest. We can't afford to lose that much so we have to stay with the trade. **Wrong**, we have already lost that much and we have to get out of the trade, although I would normally suggest placing another stop to effect this, thus giving the trade a chance. But this is something of a stopgap measure, it is easier for the suffering

Humility definitely has a high value in the markets.

trader to do this than get out outright. If the trader does not do this then a long period of suffering can ensue, sometimes going on for weeks. Eventually the pain gets so bad that it exceeds the other pain. That other pain is the pain of accepting the loss, admitting it is yours and taking it. Traders are unwilling to take a loss because they don't want to admit the loss and hope it will go away, that they will not have to confront it, and accept their own stupidity. Far better to accept we are all pretty stupid upfront, before we start to risk money, but this is something we find difficult to do. Humility definitely has a high value in the markets.

It so happens that when this point is reached it is often a major turning point in the market. So the trader feels doubly stupid. Not only has he made a big loss, by holding far too long, he also got out at just the wrong time. Incidentally the damage this does to self esteem is a problem the trader will have to deal with before he can make it, any psychological "flaw" like this will impact on trading because it is liable to create "driven" trades from time to time. I define any emotional trading as being driven as the trader has no real control. Self esteem problems can raise their head if anything threatens that already weakened self esteem, like an argument for example. What better way to make you feel better than to trade the market!

> **The market is a manifestation of human psychology.**

Back to that suffering trader who got out just at the wrong time. The market is a manifestation of human psychology. Most market participants are making emotionally driven decisions. How everyone views the market at any one time is purely within their own minds. Market extremes are reached at peaks of emotion. Fear at lows, greed at highs. Human beings are all fairly similar in many ways. If a number of us were sitting in a room and a tiger entered, we would all have very similar impulses. If there was a window we may well all rush for it. It is therefore not surprising that a peak or trough in a market will create the maximum emotion which will cause the novice trader to finally exit a losing position. Surely that extreme emotion is almost bound to have that effect, and having drawn in the last buyer or seller (in this case the novice trader) the market will reverse.

So cutting losses is not easy and is a skill to be developed, as with all market skills. But eventually we master this and then it comes time to move onto crucial skill number two, running profits. There are two obvious problems here. First, running profits is an entirely different skill from cutting losses, and indeed is almost the converse. One involves actively watching the trade and being ready to act when necessary; the other involves a more passive role, mainly involving trying not to act. The trader needs to have really learnt how to cut losses before starting to let profits run. It is a different order of skill. Running profits is not something a novice should really try to do, too hard, because it might well cause problems cutting losses and that is the foremost priority at that stage. Once the skill of cutting losses has been acquired it is the time to worry about running profits.

Running profits

The second problem is the one mentioned above about wanting to grab nice things when we see them, when we want them. We have done that all our lives, now we have to change the habits of a lifetime. It is not easy. Some methodologies overcome these difficulties. For example my option trading approach does so to an extent because it is relatively short term, often a maximum of two weeks, and I have precise goals. I sell time value and close when it has all but gone. Simple. It is far more difficult to run a futures position and it is something which has to be learnt to the core of your being. The difficulty is that markets are always testing, probing for business in either direction. You have got to be fairly stalwart to stay with it through these tests and that is a skill you have to experience to learn. You also have to have a feel for the depth of correction you are prepared to accept, and define a trend reversal you will not. Part of this is what you see when you look at a chart. Do you see the tops and bottoms, or do you see the trends? You may think this is an odd way of looking at things but it is, in fact, critical. If you see both you will probably have trouble running profits. If you see tops and bottoms then you will be programed to see tops and bottoms. If so you are liable to see them all the time, you will get out of good trending trades. This goes fairly deep. I am not saying you have to brainwash yourself, but you need to be aware of how your mind is working.

Another factor is relaxation. I have come to the conclusion that humility and relaxation are as important in trading as are Money Management, Risk Control and the rest. If you are not relaxed then you will always be tempted to take action, taking action is the enemy of running profits.

Trading selectively

The third simple rule "Trade Selectivity" is simpler in concept but is the culmination of all the work you do as a trader. You are only going to become good at this once you have served your apprenticeship and become an expert. This whole book is about that process and so I do not intend to dwell on this here at length.

Trading with the trend

Nor do I intend to say too much about trading with the trend. Indeed this is something of a truism. Trends tend to continue, that is what they do. Thus if you trade with it you are going to have much better odds in your favor. Of course there are different trends within every timescale. So first you must decide on your timescale. Then you must devise meth-

Chapter 10

SYSTEM PARAMETERS – THE THINKING BEHIND SYSTEM DESIGN

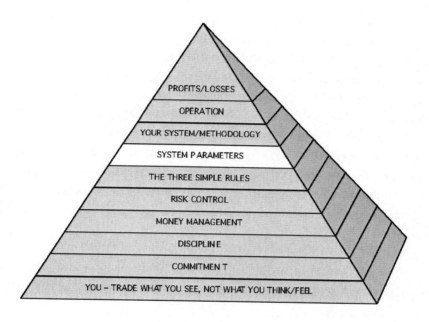

In the market there are two types of risk. There is the risk of losing money and there is the risk of losing a lot of money. As there are no free lunches you can expect the three trading vehicles which we are discussing to offer a balance against these two types or risk and this is what we find. If we buy options we have a nil risk of losing a lot of money (defined as more than your original stake) as all we can lose is what we paid for them in the first place. But if we buy options we find that we normally lose money. If we decide to write options (which I am treating as a separate trading vehicle) we find that our risk of loss is low, as option writers win most months. But when we lose we can get wiped out. This depressing process happens again, and again, and again. For novices, I believe, futures present the best balance. The risk of loss is about 50/50 (depending on your skill level) but careful use of stops and risk control (not holding at stupid times) can strictly limit your exposure to large losses (not eliminate).

So let's us look at each vehicle in turn:

Buying options

To make money this way you need to get both time and price right. You start with a severe handicap (the options premium) and this is difficult to overcome, but not impossible. However, to make money buying options you need to have reached a fairly advanced level of skill. Novice traders are attracted to them because they like the fact that the loss is limited to the amount paid, they fail to realize that that is what they will lose, most of the time. The other problem with buying options is that you have to catch a fast move, otherwise you will find that as the market moves your way, the options premium (time value) will dissipate as quickly as the intrinsic value increases. You have to be good to make money with options. If you are good then you won't need me to tell you how to do it.

Writing options

Most of my trading is done writing options. You start with a big benefit, but to keep it you have to hedge in the futures market. It is when you have to consider taking off such hedges that it can get rather complex. In Chapter 11 I discuss simple trading rules and the human brain. Complex trading is a nightmare until you are experienced. Trying to juggle naked options with hedging futures positions is far from simple and straightforward. However, this form of trading has good potential to provide good and consistent returns, but you need to learn how to do it.

Futures

Conventional wisdom is that futures are far too risky. Never trust what is generally accepted, it is almost always wrong. Futures are probably the best vehicle to go for, but only once you have understood the first lesson – cut your losses. If you follow the trading strategies outlined in this book then you will be only trading the best opportunities, getting out quickly if it goes wrong, and allowing profits to run. Do that and you have won before you even start.

Designing a system

So how do you design a system? Well, the first step is to put the structure in place. By this I mean the aim of your system. What do you want it to do? Do you want it to catch trends? Do you want to trade ranges? How much risk do you want to incur? What success ratio are you looking for?

Some of these parameters are going to affect each other. For example, if your stops are very close then your success ratio is going to be reduced. But as long as you have realistic expectations there is no reason why they cannot be met.

Having decided what you want, the next step is observation. Examine how markets behave and how you think you can take advantage of their actions. That is the key element to any system. You must divorce yourself from the psychological effects that markets have on your psyche. You have to double guess the market, because otherwise you will be losing all the time.

There are various ways of doing this. But primarily you can look to trade ranges or you can look to trade trends. The first means looking for extremes and entering when such extremes are reached. The second means looking to catch trends and entering once your system indicates that a trend is in place. You can also combine these two approaches.

In both cases you need to define your trading conditions. You need to define a range or a trend. Once you define what you are looking for, you, simultaneously, define how to catch it. You can define trends in many different ways. First you have to decide over what time frame you wish to define the trend. You must then use that time frame to give your trending signal, for example if you feel that you want to trade weekly trends then you must in some way define the trend using weekly charts. Once you have defined the trend you will have your trend indicator. So if you decide that a higher high on a weekly bar chart means that you have an uptrend then that is your indicator. Alternatively you may decide that acceptance above the previous day's value area (see Chapters 15 and 18) signifies an uptrend – again that is your trend indicator.

Incidentally I am going to concentrate on trending systems for the purposes of this chapter, but the same basic approach will apply to whatever you decide to trade, be they trends, ranges, spreads, or whatever takes your fancy.

System requirements

At this point let us list the requirements that you need to make up the entire system:

1 You need to *define your objectives.*
2 Therefrom you get your *trending signal.*
3 You must then decide on your *Money Management system* – this is critical.
4 The Money Management system tells you how much you can risk on each trade and from this you can decide on your *stop policy* and *position size.*
5 You must then decide on your *entry strategy.*
6 The next step is how to *move your stop* as the trade progresses.
7 Finally you will want an *exit strategy*, although this may simply be to wait for the stop to be hit.

So far we have covered items 1 and 2. Money Management is dealt with in Chapter 7 and I don't want to repeat this here. Suffice to say that ideally you should not risk more than 1 per cent or 2 per cent per trade with 5 per cent as the maximum, but not recommended. Otherwise you will run the risk of being wiped out.

The stop policy follows on from this. Once you know what you can risk you can work out the stop policy and the position size. However your stop policy goes to the core of your system. It is the relationship between your entry point and the stop which defines the system. To an extent this is where the magic comes in. This is the essential element which we cannot reach by logic. This is an act of creation. You must decide upon your methodology which is the heart of the system.

This particular aspect requires observation, thought, creation, and then testing. Although the actual creation must be yours there might be a few guidelines which I can usefully give. Before I do so a few words about buying systems. It is far better to develop your own system, but if you want to short cut this process then you can buy another person's system. Just make sure it has some chance of being compatible with your trading aims, and don't be suckered into buying a "black box," in fact just don't be suckered. In this context a "free" system could work out more expensive than anything else!

Time Price Opportunities

We will start with Time Price Opportunities (TPOs) (see Chapter 18). All charts are made up from these building blocks, which equate to price ticks. The building blocks themselves merely refer to the fact that as time goes by, illusory thought it may be, different prices are available and traded. Hence TPOs, a term from Peter Steidlmayer's Market Profile (MP). From TPOs you can build whatever form of chart you want. Don't be constrained by the methods you know, bar charts, point and figure, candlesticks, MP itself. Be adventurous, devise new ways of displaying the raw data (TPOs) – you do not need to stick to the ways you know and you may find a method which suits the purposes of your system much better (maybe you will be the next Steidlmayer, discovering a better way of looking at markets!). Experiment with using time in a different way, and then price. As you do so you may find that different ideas present themselves to you.

Maybe you will be the next Steidlmayer, discovering a better way of looking at markets!

Looking at price action rather than TPOs themselves we find different aspects to view. Is the action determined in one direction or the other? Has it exceeded previous highs or lows? Has it moved sharply away from previous highs or lows? Has a particular price level been sharply rejected? Has a particular price level been accepted? All these questions, and their answers, can give you a clue as to how your system might work.

Going on from price action we have all manner of indicators which present us with different forms of squiggles and dashes with which to conjure.

Out of all this information the system designer needs to choose what to use to achieve his own objectives. My own preferred "indicator" of choice is Minus Development (MD) which is generally, but not always, a spike. I like the spike because it is an extreme and the stop placed beyond the spike is relatively secure. I think systems built around spikes have a better chance of success than other systems. The placement of the stop is vitally important because if the stop is vulnerable then so is the entire system and this brings us onto the concept of data stability. Longer term data is more stable and will give you better signals; on the other side of the coin you will be forced to use much larger stops, thus either risking more or trading fewer contracts.

> **The placement of the stop is vitally important because if the stop is vulnerable then so is the entire system.**

Long-term and short-term systems

So here is the big dilemma. If you want the biggest bang for your buck you are going to be looking at short-term systems, thus using less stable data and hitting a greater number of losers. But the better systems are going to be longer term. Many traders I know are already in catch 22. They trade precisely because they haven't got much money and they see trading as a means of getting rich. Thus they are forced to look at shorter term systems, because they cannot afford to take the longer term signals, and they are also in too much of a hurry to wait for such signals in the first place. Those who are rich have great respect for their money, which is why they are rich in the first place, and will only trade in a very cautious way, meaning longer term systems, and they will have the patience to wait for the signals. Many traders have little respect for their money and until they learn that respect they are probably doomed to fail.

However the actual design of a system need not be different for longer term or shorter term purposes, except that longer term systems are likely to be trend orientated as markets tend to trend over the longer term. This might lead the system designer to thinking along two distinct lines. The first might be "to get from point 'A', where the trend begins, to point 'B' where it ends, the price must move through many points in between." So, the task will be to define such a point at which the system will enter the trend, preferably with stops beyond an extreme of sorts. The other thought might be "when the old trend ends and a new trend begins there are often similar types of price action." So, the task will be to define the type of price action to define such a turning point. By price action, I include all the various indicators, etc. and how they might behave at turning points or as trends continue.

It would be useful if readers wanted to write follow up pieces to this. That way we might get some very interesting insights to how systems may be designed. If you do, feel free to e-mail me a copy.

Putting it all together

Finally let's design a system! Our objective is to catch and stay with the big moves. We are going to use the weekly chart to determine trend. The rule will be that we must see two-weekly highs or lows taken out. So an uptrend means that two-weekly highs must be penetrated, we must also see acceptance above that second high. The stop is the last major high or low. We will also use major failed re-tests as a trading signal, as seen on 5 August 1998 on FTSE and 4 September 1998 on the S&P. Entry can either be simply when the signal comes in or you might use shorter term techniques to try and catch the move. The stop will be moved to breakeven once we are 50 points in profit and will stay there. Otherwise we will only exit when we see a signal the other way. This simple system will catch virtually all good moves. The stop is secure, and, relatively, close. It allows profits to run. It would probably only trade a few times each year, maybe just once. In fact once would be ideal, because the best trades never end, they just keep on making money.

If you like this concept then check it out on some back data over a number of markets. The last major buy signal on FTSE would have been triggered around 4990 (on the cash) in early December 1997 when the high of the week ending 21 November was taken out. The stop would originally have been at 4382, but would have quickly moved to breakeven. That trade would have take in around 780 points and the

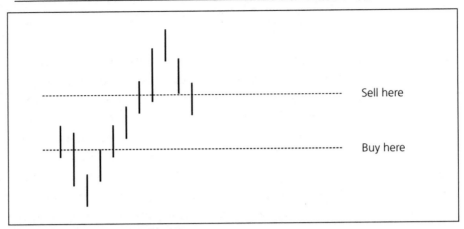

Sell here

Buy here

Fig 10.1 The *TTT* Weekly System

system would have gone short in May 1998. We now await either a
reversal signal (either by the weekly chart or by seeing a major reversal
signal) or getting stopped out. Let's call this the *TTT* Weekly System. It
is illustrated in Figure 10.1. Some of the rules above would need to be
more closely defined but my objective is to give an example of what
might work in the markets. Anything that allows big profits and takes
small losses fits the bill. In this case the initial stop was rather wide but
on the other hand the market never looked back after the signal in early
December. But you cannot judge a system on one isolated incidence.

SUMMARY

- There are primarily three types of trading vehicle with which we are concerned here. I treat buying options and writing options as two separate vehicles. The third vehicle is futures.

- System design requires the consideration of a number of key factors, including time frame, stop policy and Money Management.

- You have to decide whether to trade ranges or trends.

- You must define what you want, define what your system is designed to achieve. The major act of creation is to decide which element of market action will generate buy and sell signals.

- The stop policy is one of the most important aspects as it defines your risk/reward ratio.

- The *TTT* Weekly System is an example of what might work in the markets.

Chapter 11

SYSTEM PARAMETERS – SIMPLE TRADING RULES AND THE HUMAN BRAIN

As soon as an idea is accepted it is time to reject it.

Holbrook Jackson

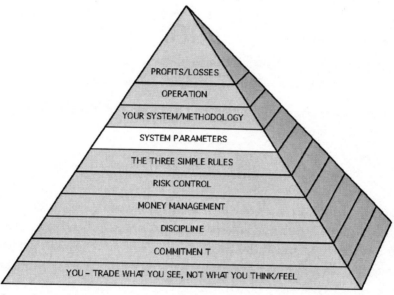

In this chapter I want to explain the trading process, explain what analysis is really for, and show how to win in the markets. You may think this a little ambitious but I have been trading for 10 years and I have learnt the truth of these matters the hard way.

There are of course two sides to trading. The first is the theory, and this is where the simple rules come in. The second is the practice and this is where the human brain (including all emotional and instinctive input) comes in. The formula is simple:

Simple Trading Rules + Human Brain = Chaos and Confusion

Anyone who has ever traded knows the truth of this formula.

So here come the simple rules. If your trading approach lets profits run and cuts losses short and if it achieves a 50 per cent hit rate then overall you will win. This is clearly so. For each profit there will be a loss, but as profits are allowed to run they will average a larger sum than the losses, which are always kept small.

The purpose of analysis (technical or fundamental) is not to analyze markets, it is to build your system/trading approach. This is not to denigrate Technical Analysis because building your system is an essential step to success. The reason I know that you need a system is because of that formula on the previous page. A system does produce simple trading rules. Anything else is going to be more complicated. I might summarize this as:

If Simple Trading Rules + Human Brain = Chaos and Confusion
***Then* Complex Trading Rules + Human Brain = ?**

That question mark is not pleasant – I have lived it during the first part of my trading career.

Systems

So the trader has a clear goal: to produce a system which will, overall, give an edge. A 50 per cent hit rate is a good target, but you can get away with less than that and still win, if profits run enough. This is where the analysis comes in – to produce that system. Neither letting profits run, nor cutting losses short is that simple (see Chapter 9) but they can be learnt. So this need not be a big problem.

Personally I do not like statistical type indicators and for my own trading I have developed systems based on Peter Steidlmayer's Market Profile. The concepts of "Value," "Minus Development," and "Acceptance" are like a breath of fresh air after some of the rubbish I have wasted my time on over the last decade. These important concepts are dealt with exhaustively in this book.

A quick word about "random" systems, or more correctly "random-entry" systems. I have often heard it said that random systems work – i.e. just toss a coin to decide on entry criteria. I have not tested this theory, but there would seem a logical flaw. I would accept that a random-entry system with no stops would most likely win 50 per cent of the time. But this would achieve nothing because the profits and losses would probably become equivalent over time – and commissions would probably kill you. Once you start to use stops it is likely (guaranteed) that your hit rate would drop from 50 per cent. Forgetting the psychological problems of trading a system taking loads of losses, the arithmetic may still kill you.

For my own systems I accept the "logic of the stop." The key is to keep losses small, therefore the key item is the relationship between the entry point and the stop. This is where Minus Development (MD) comes in – my stops are always placed beyond MD. I want to avoid excessive philosophy within this chapter but it is often (usually?) what is not there that is important rather than what is. This is illustrated by Sherlock Holmes and "the dog that didn't bark." Great musicians say that it is the spaces between the notes which are crucial, not the notes themselves. MD is the absence of development. Steidlmayer's work is the making of Chaos into Order. The bell curve does this. Development takes place when the market spends some time at certain price levels. MD occurs when the market spends little or no time at a particular price – it occurs when that price level is rejected.

The stop level controls your risk. It is the ratio between risk and reward which governs how successful your system allows you to be. However again I digress, the important point to realize is that it is not difficult to produce a system that will give you a winning edge.

The human brain

But that is only stage 1. The difficult bit is using it! This is where the human brain comes in.

In the excellent article by Tony Plummer (see Appendix 2) mention is made of the "triune" brain. Briefly this comprises three parts, what we might call the instinctive, emotional and thoughtful parts. Once we introduce the human brain to any equation we introduce all three parts. The thoughtful part is useful within the trading context. However the other parts are not always so. Trading is a highly charged business. Money, lots of it, is involved. There is risk of loss and potentially large rewards. Most traders overtrade, immediately putting themselves under substantial psychological pressure. This is not surprising because if you overtrade you are likely to be wiped out – it is a logical certainty. All this brings the instinctive and emotional parts of the brain into action, often frenzied action. This is not helpful for trading. They make you do the wrong thing at the wrong time, they make you join the herd, they shake you out of good positions, they do everything they can to guarantee that you lose.

> *Trading is a highly charged business. Money, lots of it, is involved.*

The human brain has its part to play – that is in designing the system and then monitoring its performance. But whilst the system is active it should be left alone. But that is what, ultimately, is so difficult.

At the start of this chapter I said that I wanted to explain the trading process, explain what analysis is really for, and show how to win in the markets. Let me end by summarizing these three. The trading process is to adopt a low risk strategy. Losses must be kept low (1 per cent or 2 per cent of capital is a good guideline) and profits must be allowed to run (otherwise you will never cover your losses). A good system will do this whilst still giving you a 50 per cent plus hit rate – yes, you are still going to lose around half the time! Not easy for those who have a deep felt respect for their hard earned cash.

Analysis is for the purpose of developing your system, end of story. You win by learning how to control your emotions and instincts so that you can follow your system – that takes experience but I believe that the process can be short circuited if you know what the problems are – but then I am an optimist.

SUMMARY

- The basic equation is that:
  Simple Trading Rules + the Human Brain = Chaos and Confusion
  This is primarily due to the workings of the triune brain.

- More complex rules become extremely difficult to operate, especially for novices.

- The logic of the stop determines the risk/reward of your approach.

Chapter 12

DEVELOPING YOUR METHODOLOGY

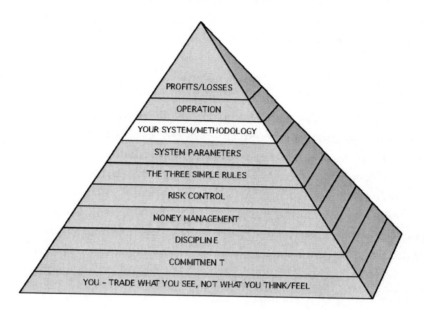

PROFITS/LOSSES
OPERATION
YOUR SYSTEM/METHODOLOGY
SYSTEM PARAMETERS
THE THREE SIMPLE RULES
RISK CONTROL
MONEY MANAGEMENT
DISCIPLINE
COMMITMEN T
YOU - TRADE WHAT YOU SEE, NOT WHAT YOU THINK/FEEL

This is perhaps the key section to this book because it is your methodology that ultimately determines whether you win or lose. It is equally vital that you have the discipline to stick to your methodology, but you cannot even begin to do that until you have the methodology itself.

I cannot give you *your* methodology. I can make suggestions, I can put forward examples, as I do in this book, but ultimately you must devise a system which is your own, because you have to be able to follow it. Therefore to be useful it has to accord to your personality.

I cannot stress this point enough. You will not be able to use another trader's successful system for a number of reasons. You must first define your own personality as it relates to the market. You will find there are some things you can do and some things you can't. You will find you have certain strengths and certain weaknesses. The key is to develop a methodology that makes the most of your strengths and minimizes your weaknesses. But there are other factors to consider. One is time frame. There is no point in trying to trade intra-day (i.e. getting in and out as the markets move in the course of a single day) if your own preference is to take a much longer view. This is an obvious example of why one trader's methodology may not suit you.

So before I go into a few examples of methodologies I will set out some of the parameters.

Time frame

Do you want to trade intra-day, daily, weekly or monthly? To an extent this means do you want to catch market moves which extend over such periods, although another way of putting it is that you might look for the turning points that correspond with your chosen time frame. Once you have made this decision you then know what you wish to look for and then you can tailor your analysis to achieve just that. So already you have taken a step forwards. Incidentally a methodology might include a number of different strategies including different time frames. This is not meant to be a "tick one only" type of approach – although it may suit you best to choose just one.

Trading type

There are many ways of trading markets. The most usual is a "directional" approach looking to take profits as a market moves in a direction that benefits your particular position. However, a strategy of writing straddles (writing both put and call options at the same striker), for example, does best when markets do not move. Arbitrage is another approach looking for short-term anomalies and capitalizing on them. Then there is hedging, spread trading, and a wide range of derivative products. If you go for a directional approach then you still have to choose whether to trade with stocks, warrants, options or futures. And then you have to decide whether you want to go long or short of these instruments, although often you will want to do both.

Analysis type

Most people approach analysis in the wrong way. They come into contact with one particular technique, be it Elliott, Gann, MACD, or whatever. They then get to know how this technique works and then they start to use it. If you think about it this is bound to happen, but it is putting the cart before the horse. Any type of analysis is designed to answer particular questions. A doctor examining a patient looks for symptoms and then decides to do further analysis to answer the outstanding questions. A doctor doesn't become an expert in feet, and then do foot analysis whatever problem

> *Decide how you want to trade, decide what opportunities you want to exploit, then choose your analysis methods around that.*

the patient may have. But this is how most technical analysts approach the situation. They become expert in a particular technique and regardless of how they should be trading (to suit themselves) they use that technique. This is particularly a problem for traders starting out because they may know no more than that one technique.

This is another way in which "analysis" is a negative. It is often used as the foundation stone of the methodology but it should just be one factor. The way to approach this is the other way round. Decide how you want to trade, decide what opportunities you want to exploit, *then* choose your analysis methods around that. Avoid the use of well-known techniques in well-known ways, because the majority do that, and the majority lose. You want to do something different – you want to be a winner.

My own view is that most analysis is a waste of time. Most successful traders look for set-ups. By this I mean that they work out a methodology which triggers an entry point when a certain type of action is seen. If the market meets their criterion they act – if it does not they do not.

Money Management (MM)

MM is covered in more detail in Chapter 7. To explain the purpose of MM, let me give you a simple example. Let us say you have the best entry and exit methodology (see below) in the world. You have a 99 per cent success rate. Yes out of every 100 trades, 99 make money – you can't go wrong! But you have the worst possible MM system. You bet the ranch on each trade. So what happens, you probably become a multi-millionaire, but then that 1 in a 100 chance comes along and you lose – **everything**! An MM system is designed to do two things. Of paramount importance is that you never get wiped out, the second function is to maximize your returns.

There are some very complex formulae for working out the optimum MM but they all depend on knowing your hit rate. This is a big problem not least because even if you do arrive at a figure for your hit rate it is going to be historic and not necessarily representative of future performance. For this, and other reasons, we are not going to go into such formulae.

Of paramount importance is that you never get wiped out, the second function is to maximize your returns.

However, I will repeat one observation I saw on one of these formulae known as "Optimal F." A trader who lost said "I've been Optimally F'd!" It doesn't sound too pleasant.

Instead we want to stick to the basics. There is one main criterion which MM decides for you and that is how much you risk on any one trade and this is a factor of two variables, position size and stop point. To give a simple example you might decide that you will risk no more than 5 per cent of your capital on any one position. If that is 5 per cent flat you must then make 20 losses in a row to wipe you out, but if the 5 per cent is worked out on reducing capital it will take more trades, after 10 trades you would still have £6000 left, assuming a starting level of £10 000.

In working out your MM system you have to have regard to the following:

1 The amount of your capital.
2 The success or otherwise of your overall methodology – yes this is a reflexive process. Incidentally if your methodology is not successful – change it!
3 The relationship between the amount of your losses and the amount of your profits.

4 Expected maximum drawdown (x2?).
5 The number of positions you might have open at any one time.
6 The type of trading you do.
7 The potential in the market for killer moves.

MM is an absolute essential for trading success.

Risk control (RC)

RC is covered in more detail in Chapter 8. RC can be said to be part of
MM but it also has a separate function. Your MM system will look after
you to an extent but sometimes the market will force you into a bigger
loss than you had expected. For example you may have decided to exit
a position if FTSE fell below 5700, say. But
what happens if FTSE gap opens to 5650?   *If something threatens your*
Clearly your loss is correspondingly big-   *survival you have to act.*
ger. RC is a method of trying to avoid this
sort of situation. So if the market looks like it is becoming more volatile
you may want to reduce or even close positions. Of course this can be
subjective and you may well be doing the wrong thing at the wrong
time, as the market tends to make us do. But the key consideration in the
market is survival, if something threatens your survival you have to act.

Entry methodology (EM)

Analysis is a means to an end, and no more. That end is EM and ExM
(see below). It is when you know when to enter and exit that you have
a clear methodology. All the other factors translate into these two moves
which ultimately define your success or failure. EM is the easy bit.

Exit methodology (ExM)

ExM is the more difficult bit and understandably so because it is the exit
which actually crystalizes your profit or loss. At this point I will say a few
words about my own methodology. I write (sell) options and then look
to hedge positions, as need be, with futures positions. I very rarely close

the written options (other than for a few pence) because the whole game is to take out the time value. This process is complete at expiration, or earlier assignment. So I avoid exit on this approach, although I have a general rule to close out positions once they become very cheap, i.e. 15 points or so. When I hedge with the futures, that is also easy, as it is an entry and the only difficulty is when to take off the hedge, i.e. the ExM.

To complete this chapter I set out an interview with an institutional trader which serves to illustrate many of these points.

Interview with an institutional trader

In doing this interview it has been gratifying to find that many of the principles with which this individual works are those which regularly appear in the pages of my newsletter (and of this book). The individual I interviewed wishes to remain anonymous, for a variety of reasons, and I, of course, will respect his wishes.

First let me say that this individual does not work on a trading floor and is not surrounded by colleagues doing the same thing. He works by himself and his management company is contracted by institutions who wish him to trade their money. He prefers his solitude because he does not get swayed to the same extent by market sentiment; but there are negatives, in particular, not seeing the order flow and not getting the news and the stories as quickly.

Requirements for success in the market

It comes as no surprise that discipline is a key to his approach. He says that before you can succeed in markets there are a number of precise requirements:

1 First you need a method which differentiates between price and value, thus highlighting good trading opportunities. Analysis is required to construct such a method but then becomes of less importance. It is critical that such a method is understood by the trader and suits his/her personality.

2 Second, whatever the method, you need to be able to get out when you are wrong without losing a lot of money. The problem many

private traders face is that they trade on their opinions and are prepared to lose a lot before they will change those opinions.

3 Third you need to know where you would get out before you enter a trade. This confirms that the amount you can lose is a factor to which you must pay a lot of attention. He will not take a trade which does not offer a fairly close get out. With reference to FTSE this means around 40 points. However stops are not simple and are not placed in the market. He will want to see the market trading at his "stop" level and also that it stays there before exiting. A spike to that level will not do it. However he also uses a "Money Management" stop beyond the other stop which is used automatically – however this is placed a "safe" distance away.

4 The overall approach needs to be fairly flexible as it needs to be able to handle changing market conditions.

These four requirements tie in fairly well with the "trading rules" I have published from time to time and readers can see that all the essentials are present.

The Money Management approach is fairly straightforward. He feels that he never wants to be down as much as 25 per cent, because people tend to remove funds if faced with a loss of that size. He then divides this sum into 10 and that is the amount he is prepared to risk on any one position. So if he were trading £1 million the amount of risk allocated to any one trade would be £25 000 or 2.5 per cent. With the FTSE futures he might therefore trade 30–40 contracts (this was when FTSE was £25 per point, the figures would be correspondingly larger at the current rate of £10 per point) allowing for a stop 40 points or less away from entry levels. However this will vary with market volatility and position size will be reduced in very volatile conditions. At market extremes he might increase position size because of the "added value" such a trade offers. He reckons that this approach means that his risk of being wiped out is less than 1 per cent. It also keeps drawdowns down to acceptable levels. His methodology is on average 55–60 per cent correct and he finds that a maximum of four or five losing trades in a row is the most that can be expected – thus maximum drawdown using this approach has been around 12 per cent. Since he developed this strategy he has not had a losing year and some years have shown truly impressive gains. He started trading in 1985 and his aim is to make 20 per cent per annum – a figure I have often mentioned as a good benchmark for traders.

That sets the scene for the type of environment within which a trader ought to operate. The controls are not external, they are imposed on this trader through self discipline – which must always be the case, especially for the private trader who has no alternative. The only external control is that the brokers he uses know what his maximum position sizes are and he is unable to exceed those limits, not that he would want to. His approach is longer term, and he says that it is important for every trader to define his time frame. On average he will only trade one market once a month. As such he will expect losing months and these do not concern him unduly. Losing trades are part of his (our) business.

> **Losing trades are part of his (our) business.**

Type of trading

We will now turn to the type of trading which this trader does, albeit that the overall structure would not necessarily change whatever his approach might be. The trader is essentially a directional swing trader, trying to catch the more important moves and using futures to profit from such moves. He uses both technicals and fundamentals and his basic approach is adapted from the basic principles of market logic, updated in view of modern market distribution developments. He does not look to get in at the highs or the lows but will try to stay with a trade for as long as it remains valid. His approach is based around his exit strategy which he believes is far more important. This is clearly the case because it is the exit that determines whether you win or lose, and how much, on any position. He is surprised by the relative amount of time that traders, even institutional traders, spend on entry strategies. Everybody is obsessed with analysis techniques giving buy or sell signals but the key is when to get out, not in. He uses his approach on a variety of different markets, without changing it, but concentrates on a few markets. These being US, UK and German equity and bond futures – but he does not like to have more than two positions open at any one time. This fact further reduces his overall risk of loss because of his Money Management rules. He believes that market moves are basically unpredictable and never has a view as to where a market may go – he also believes that the obsession with market predictions is one of the major causes for failure in this business. However, he does believe that there are methodologies which allow a trader to take advantage of the fact that a market price is currently above or below "value." His methodology is designed to achieve just that.

As an example, a jobber defines value as the last tick. The jobber will then look to buy below that tick and sell over it. So if the last tick was 6005 the jobber's bid/offer spread may be 6004/6006. By doing this the jobber is trying to trade at an advantage to "value" – see Figure 12.1.

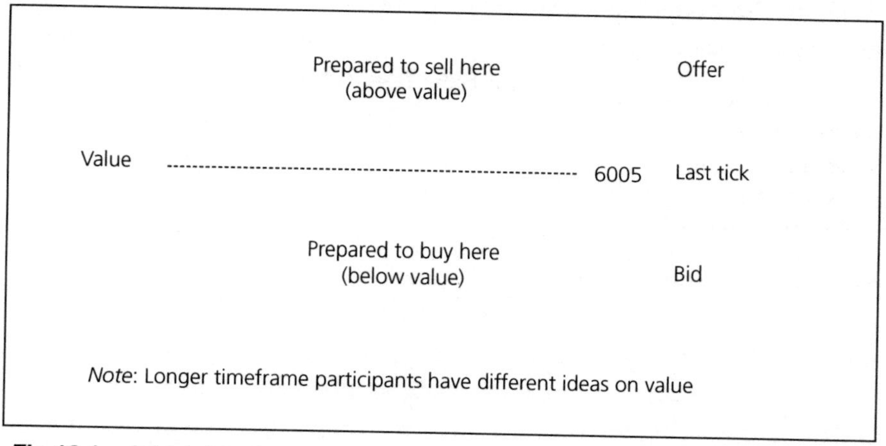

	Prepared to sell here (above value)	Offer
Value	-------- 6005	Last tick
	Prepared to buy here (below value)	Bid

Note: Longer timeframe participants have different ideas on value

Fig 12.1   Jobber's value

Our trader is trying to do just that, but over a longer time frame.

He raised an interesting point concerning time, which he believes is another factor that most traders undervalue. Following on from the fact that only the minority win he likes to trade at a price which is only briefly available. If the price then becomes widely available, because the market trades at that level for a longer period of time, it weakens the strength of the trade. For example if he sees the market open at a certain level and then move rapidly away from that level, as the market rejects the opening price, that encourages his view that he has got in at a good price, if he had traded at that point. But if the market went back to that level it would reduce the value of his entry. This point only relates to attractive prices. After a strong rally prices will be high, which is not too attractive to buyers but might be to sellers (it's always easy to sell at "high" prices within an uptrend) – but it is only if the seller can capture a price which then quickly becomes unobtainable to another seller that he can say he has received an advantage not available to other than a few people.

Having entered a position he will either be stopped out fairly quickly because the market triggers his stop methodology or the position will go into profit. He then adopts a trailing stop approach – although the stop levels are chosen using the same methodology and stops will be operative in the same way.

He considers his whole approach opportunistic in that he is always looking to trade at an advantage. If he is stopped out of a trade which he feels has further to go then he might well re-enter but probably with fewer contracts. He will certainly miss a trade if the stop level is too far away because he finds that there are plenty of trades which do meet his criteria.

> **One of the keys for trading success is the ability to take trades when you need to.**

He doesn't like mechanical systems for two reasons. First because although they may catch good moves they also deliver a lot of dross in the interim. Second because those who use them often don't fully understand how they work, thus making them virtually inoperative.

Turning to the all important question of psychology he avoids a lot of the problems traders can encounter because first he understands his approach, and second he has proved that it is effective. He believes that one of the keys for trading success is the ability to take trades when you need to. Many traders end up undergoing a dialogue with themselves before trading which is self defeating. If you have a strategy then you should use it – assuming it is worthwhile (if it is not you should not use it). Things are going to go wrong from time to time so what is the point of allowing this fact to hinder your trading.

He likens trading to a sport which has to be done without reference to external considerations. So, like an athlete competing in the Olympic games, he believes it is important to remain detached from external considerations, family, friends, or finance for example, and to remain focused on the task in hand. This also means trading in isolation from the possible consequences of that action in financial terms.

Another factor which he feels adversely affects the private trader is the compulsion to trade – i.e. taking more trades than your method might indicate. But this would be counter productive as it would mean taking trades which do not fully meet your criteria thus diluting the effectiveness of the system.

Finally he finds the views of others useful, but only in a contrarian way – he always makes his own decisions and is not swayed by the views of others. I have for some years been looking to devise a contrarian indicator and I have now decided how I am going to do this. I will be doing a separate feature on this in a future issue of *TTT*.

To conclude, our trader sees the market as a balancing mechanism, which it undoubtedly is, and his methodology is designed to catch trades which take advantage of imbalances within the system. From this you can see that there is a clear logic behind his approach, that he carries out his methodology in a disciplined fashion, and that his Money Management rules give him the edge he needs to make it all work.

SUMMARY

- Developing your methodology requires a consideration of the following:
  1 Time frame.
  2 Type of trading etc.
  3 Type of analysis.
  4 Money management.
  5 Risk control.
  6 Entering and exit.

- I set out an interview with an institutional trader which underlines many points, including many in this book, to which traders must have regard.

Chapter 13

OPERATION

If you can keep your head when all about are losing theirs, perhaps you have misunderstood the situation.

Anonymous (graffiti)

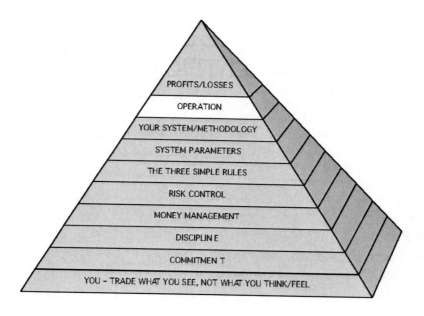

So far we have dealt with the philosophy that needs to be put in place if you are going to be successful. I am not saying this is the only philosophy that will work, but it is that which I find useful. I would remind you that "nothing is cast in stone," "there is no absolute truth," all we can work with are "useful lies" – hypotheses which stand or fall solely on whether they are found to work in the marketplace.

Now we turn our attention to actual trading situations. There are many such approaches, as many as there are different traders. Each trader has his own winning approach. Many never find theirs, allowing themselves to be knocked out of the market for one reason or another: overtrading, bad Money Management, lack of commitment, lack of effort, and so on. Remember we are always responsible for *everything* that ever happens to us, from birth onwards. This is an important "useful lie" to start off with. So at this point we may diverge even further from what is useful for you.

The set-up

When it comes to operation I go though a distinct thought process. The primary key is the set-up. I do not worry about trading systems or trading signals at all until I see something which tells me there is a good chance that we have a trend in place. It is only then that I start to worry about which system is the most useful to trade the move. This is a big departure from the way many use systems. Many just follow system rules, but the reality is that the market is almost random when looked at from a mathematical point of view, so many systems do not achieve very much, they just seek to churn your account. I believe you need something better. Certainly you need a methodology because if you do not have something which tells you what to do, you will never know when you are trading emotionally rather than with the whole of your being. You need to go through a phase when you know precisely what you should be doing so that you can correct "harmful" personality traits. But there are many phases in the trader's life (see the 55 Steps in Chapter 2). All these phases can be likened to stepping stones on the route to your eventual success.

> **I do not worry about trading systems or trading signals at all until I see something which tells me there is a good chance that we have a trend in place.**

Set-ups come in various shapes and sizes but let us itemize the mental process:

1 Identify the set-up.
2 Decide on a certain trade (long or short).
3 Observe action as to which trading system is most appropriate.
4 See the signal.
5 Consider stop points/risk parameters.

6 Put on the position.

7 Monitor the trade.

8 Place stops, if appropriate (see Chapter 15). Personally I prefer to only place "long stops" which are unlikely to be hit. In the early phase I may exit very quickly if I do not see the action I am looking for.

9 At this point there are three main possibilities. It may go wrong fairly quickly and you are stopped out. You congratulate yourself about your perfect trading and feel good about it. Or it may go well from the very start and you can start to raise stops and become comfortable as the risk of loss gets lower and lower. Or it may meander around, in which case you may decide to exit in an "anticipatory" style. If so be sure to re-enter if the trade criteria remain valid. This is a key point.

The set-ups I use are to do with extremes and the signals I look for are failed re-tests, failed breaks and failed extensions. The first two are fully discussed in Chapter 22. The latter is my favorite signal and involves a market giving a solid buy or sell signal and then doing a whip-saw move back beyond the extreme. Then the true reversal comes in. I find this happens a lot at key peak and troughs.

Problems with operation

I said earlier that I would look at some of the problems traders have with operation. Some of these go deep, very deep, and the solution may require the services of a trading coach or psychologist (see Chapter 16). But we can look at some pointers.

Of course, we have already covered some of the ground. Most traders trade far too often, because they are emotionally driven. But those who cannot pull the trigger often have more

> *Most traders trade far too often, because they are emotionally driven.*

intractable problems. These problems may be simple fear, they may have to do with complex belief systems (trading isn't real work, for example) which paralyze them, or they may have resulted from an earlier experience, perhaps in childhood, which is deeply buried within the subconscious.

A good book on neuro-linguistic-programming (NLP) helps with belief systems, and this is a much cheaper option than employing a psychologist. But you need not go straight to a trading psychologist, although it may save time, as any local NLP practitioner may prove helpful. It all rather depends on what the problem may be.

If it is fear then a simple strategy may help:

1 First paper trade for a while to build up your confidence in your system. If you haven't got a system then it is perhaps better you don't pull the trigger.
2 Whilst paper trading rehearse phoning your broker for real.
3 Then find a friend or colleague to whom you can place your orders on a fictitious basis. There are also brokers in the US who offer a similar service.
4 Then phone the broker for real and start to trade for real.

This process may not work, but it should serve to pinpoint the problem with more accuracy and it is always a good idea to improve your confidence in your system.

As a general rule any problem should be viewed as a gift. The reason is that the problem bears with it its own solution, and this can be immensely rewarding. This is why I prefer not to classify news as "good" or "bad." Looked at this way you are immediately uplifted and far more likely to view the problem as the challenge it truly is. At the same time you are far less likely to get bogged down with the problem itself.

Further, all problems yield up their gifts (solutions) when subjected to careful analysis, remedial action (including rehearsal), feedback, further analysis, etc. The solution may prove radical but that may be the best possible thing. In the process you may also get to review your belief systems in full, and that is no bad thing.

One simple technique which may help consists of four questions; These are:

1 What do I want?
2 How am I going to get it?
3 What will I then have? Describe your expected emotions.
4 What will I then want? This is a repeat of question "1" and you then repeat the sequence until you get to the "correct" answer.

By going through this loop you can learn a lot, you can also reach a moment of "nothingness" which is what all the great mystics and sages down the ages have sought.

SUMMARY

- Nothing in the trading environment is set in stone. All we can work with are useful lies – hypotheses which stand or fall on your results.

- I go through a distinct mental process when entering a trade. This is detailed.

- Some traders find problems with operation, but there are ways to minimize these or at least to pinpoint the problem area.

- Problems always bring with them their solutions and should thus be viewed as gifts.

Chapter 14

THE WHOLE STRUCTURE = PROFIT/LOSS

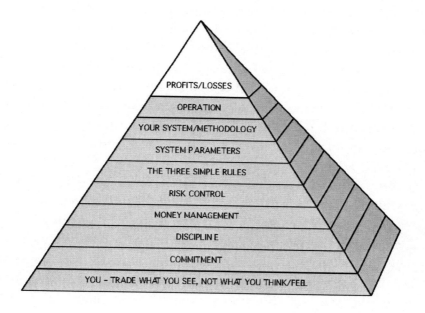

PROFITS/LOSSES
OPERATION
YOUR SYSTEM/METHODOLOGY
SYSTEM PARAMETERS
THE THREE SIMPLE RULES
RISK CONTROL
MONEY MANAGEMENT
DISCIPLINE
COMMITMENT
YOU - TRADE WHAT YOU SEE, NOT WHAT YOU THINK/FEEL

We have now discussed the Trading Pyramid in detail and covered all of the preceding levels before the final level "Profit/Loss." The final level is extremely simple, it is merely your results. But it is also critical and defines the entire structure. If you are making money on a consistent basis then you have achieved a sound structure, your pyramid is well constructed. If you are making losses then it is not. But even if you are making money do not make the mistake of thinking that you have reached the end of the road. There is no real end to this road. There is always scope for further improvement. Trading is a true life experience. In fact I find that many situations made clear by trading logic apply equally well in the real world.

There are three questions all traders need to know the answers to:

1 Why do most traders lose in the markets?
2 How can you win?
3 How do we get from losing to winning?

The answers have been dealt with in this book. To summarize they are:

1 Most lose because they are operating in a big negative sum game and they are behaving emotionally within that environment.
2 We can win by following the structure of The Trading Pyramid.
3 There are various ways of describing this process. The Traders' Evolution and the 55 steps in Chapter 2 are two such. A third is the process from emotional trading to mechanical trading to intuitive (or expert) trading. This is quite an important process within the context of the pyramid. Initially we all start trading emotionally, although we would probably deny it to our dying breath and are unlikely to realize that this is the case. Indeed the first big step is to realize that we are trading emotionally. In this context the very reason we are in the market in the first place can be our own worst enemy. Again traders rarely start to trade for the reasons they think they are trading. A typical scenario is that someone has succeeded in a profession or in business and is looking for a new challenge. Maybe he/she is a little bored with the status quo. Maybe that boredom is the real reason for trading - again this is subconscious. Guess what? When such people get bored they will be driven to trade. Such times do not necessarily correspond with a low risk trading opportunity. The same is true of those with low self esteem problems, ego problems, compulsive behavior problems, and we might go through the entire long list of all the emotional drivers which traders may experience. It is when you start to use a mechanical approach that you can start to see that you are doing other than you ought to do, then you can start to work out why. That is when you can start to make real progress. I realize I am repeating myself but this step is so crucial to success!

In this sense the pyramid is truly an organic living structure. Each level offers feedback to other levels. Once you start to learn more about **you** you can start to adjust all the levels of the pyramid to suit that **you**. That way you reach an approach which is truly tailor made and in which you can become expert/intuitive. I do not believe that mechanical trading is an end in itself, but it is a critical step along the way. It is when you have a quasi (or fully) mechanical approach in which you are an expert, so that you can intuitively deselect certain trades, that you will find the money really homing in on **you**. It is to this end which this book is directed.

SUMMARY

- Your results are the only guide to whether your pyramid is well constructed.

- I list three important questions that all traders need to answer and understand:
  1 Why do most traders lose?
  2 How can you win?
  3 How do you get from one (losing) to the other (winning)?

- Feedback within the pyramid is a key factor making the pyramid a living organic structure.

Chapter 15

STOPS AND ACCEPTANCE

Are stops necessary?

The first question any trader must ask is "do I need stops?" Stops are very much a two-edged sword, they do a lot of good, but there is a fairly high price to pay. I might be cynical and say that most traders should not use stops. That way they will get wiped out far more quickly and it would save a lot of time and bother.

However my true answer to that question is that I need stops and could not function without them. Partly this is because I trade off chart patterns. There is no fundamental basis for my trading other than market action. When I take a signal, like a failed retest for example, then I must exit when that pattern is destroyed. Always there is a price level at which the pattern ceases to have any meaning, then I exit. But there is more to it then simply that. My whole trading approach is based on risking no more than 1 or 2 per cent per trade. I simply cannot do that without stops. Thus I conclude that stops are essential, for me.

But they may not be essential for you. I recall reading about one of the top traders in *Market Wizards*. This trader had an enormous bond position in place which went substantially against him for many months. In the past I have used this as an example of when you may be able to get away without using stops. My logic at the time went long the lines that if you were one of the best fundamental traders in the world, and if you had a vast amount of money at your disposal, and if you had the mental fortitude to run those sorts of losses, then you need not use stops.

I want to examine that statement more carefully because, although it is not the whole story, it does have something to offer. There are three distinct points:

1 To avoid using stops, and I include mental stops in this, you have really got to trade on the basis of some view. Fundamentally or tech-

nically (or both) your stance can be that you will get out when your analysis is proven wrong. Unfortunately this may never happen. To give a technical example, if you sell a market because it is over-bought, you may discover to your consternation that it can get very much more over-bought over long periods of time. But if you are a good analyst and have thought out your approach and if you have the track record to back up your views and give you confidence, then you may choose not to use stops because that approach works for you.

2 But if you do not have enough money to run a large loss then you are taking a big risk. The market may just go too far for you. You may be dead right but you will still be dead. This is a key reason why I believe stops are essential. Certainly essential during the learning period when traders rarely have much clue what they are really involved with.

3 But if you find, despite being an excellent analyst and having pots of money that you just cannot take it psychologically, then you have to use stops.

There are various types of stop and they do not need to be automatic. At this point I must instill a **wealth warning**: if you are an inexperienced trader do not rely on mental stops, they can seriously damage your wealth. Some experienced traders have the same problem. When starting ensure you put your stops in the market at the same time you enter a trade.

> **If you are an inexperienced trader do not rely on mental stops.**

Different rules apply at different times in this game. During the initial phase your goal is to learn the business whilst minimizing the cost of doing so. Only later can you start to experiment with more advanced stop policies.

Stop approaches

So here is a list of a number of different stop approaches you may think of adopting:

1 The simple "in the market" fixed stop point.
2 The simple "in the brain" fixed stop point – i.e. the mental stop.
3 A time stop.
4 A stop point based on the concept of "acceptance," see below.
5 A rising stop.
6 A falling stop.
7 A stop point that makes you reconsider the position but not necessarily exit.
8 A Money Management stop.
9 A long stop.
10 A complex stop combining one or more of the above.

In addition to this list, which is not meant to be exhaustive, there are different types of stop orders that can be placed in the market itself, and these vary between the various exchanges. So the issue can get somewhat complex. However, complex is merely another word for there being a lot of options (at least in this context) so do not be deterred. The key, as ever, is to decide what you want and then to go out and do it, having first ascertained that it is possible.

Acceptance

Now a word about "acceptance," a concept that might repay the cost of this book many times over. In Chapter 20 I discuss "spiky" action. Price spikes are seen all the time in markets and they do two things: they stop out a load of traders and they give, often, a good indication of the trend. Thus you do not want to be stopped out by price spikes because they often confirm the very position they are, simultaneously, stopping you out of. The solution to this problem is "acceptance," but there are no free lunches, it comes at a price.

Acceptance is the converse of rejection. It is perhaps easier to explain rejection first. Let us say that FTSE has strong support at 4600 (or the S&P 500 strong support at 923.00). The market moves below these levels, but instantly moves back up again. Let's assume we see lows at 4597 on FTSE and at 922.90 on the S&P. Strong rallies ensue. That is rejection and it is a strong buy signal if the buying response is strong enough, a mere blip back above support is not enough. But if we have long positions in place we do not want to "lose" them through such a price spike. If we had market stops in place at 5898 on FTSE and at 1119.95 on the S&P we would be stopped out. But if we waited for price to be accepted below these key levels we would not. The above example is a clear case of rejection, within minutes the market has rejected the area below the key levels and is back up once again. If we were to see the price stay below these levels for an hour and a half and indeed to accelerate lower, we would have a clear case of acceptance. Figures 15.1 and 15.2 illustrate this against a bar chart and a market profile chart. But there is a grey area in between. It is up to each trader to clarify where acceptance begins and rejection ends and this comes down to your approach. Personally I find much beyond the obvious rejection quite difficult and rarely do I stay with a position more than 10 minutes if price is below my stop. You could say that for me rejection ends after 10 minutes and acceptance begins. Traders must decide for themselves what is best for their own trading. In terms of Market Profile this is all tied in with Minus Development and Development. A price spike in MP terms is defined as no more than two 30 minute bars (or strings of TPOs). Acceptance can be defined as development below the key level. Development takes three 30 minute bars (or strings of TPOs). So if we see price below the key level for more than one hour we have acceptance.

The beauty of this is that we can stay with trades that go a long way. So the upside potential of this technique is large. The cost is that if we are stopped out we generally get a worse price. So you must weigh the risk (that extra cost) against the reward (those additional profits). But bear in mind what a low risk opportunity this is. The cost is always very low, the potential is often huge. So I recommend you adopt this in your trading. But this is not for novices, you need to be sure you can and will get out when you need to.

Now let's get back to that bond trader who was interviewed in *Market Wizards.* I said that my initial thoughts were not the whole story. The next stage of my thinking was that it still made no sense for this individual not to use stops because if he had done he could have re-entered at a higher level. However I now realize that this is also a

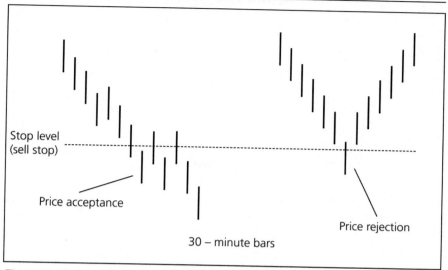

Fig. 15.1 Acceptance and rejection – price bars

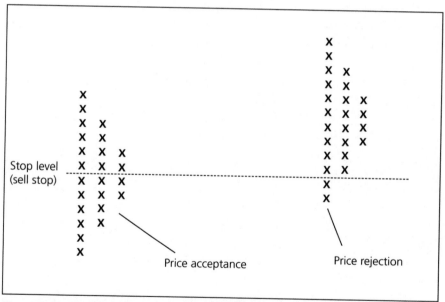

Fig. 15.2 Acceptance and rejection – Market Profile

Chapter 16

A TRADING COACH?

If you think education is expensive, try ignorance!

Derek Bok

I consider trading skills to be one of the most difficult skills to acquire, yet how many traders take on a coach to help them with their trading? If we were to talk about golf, or tennis, or sailing, or most other activities, then we would hardly think twice about taking on someone to help make it work for us, but trading, no, that seems to be different. Of course trading coaches are not cheap, but in my experience they are a lot cheaper than the losses which many make in the markets.

> *Trading coaches are not cheap, but in my experience they are a lot cheaper than the losses which many make in the markets.*

It is there that this situation becomes so absurd. It is not difficult to make money in the markets, but there are many things you need to learn (and also many things you need to "unlearn"). You will learn these through trading yourself and through reading material like this book , my newsletters and the books we recommend, but that is not enough. It is learning to *do* what you learn intellectually, that ultimately proves so difficult.

Those who play golf know the problem fairly well. It is one thing to know how you are meant to do the perfect golf swing, it is quite another to actually do it in the heat of the moment. It is the same with trading – knowing what you should do is not enough. That is where the coach comes in, he or she helps you not only to know what you should do, but actually to do it.

The benefits of working with a coach

There are a number of such coaches. Adrienne Toghraie, Van Tharp and Mark Douglas are three I am aware of. I also do some coaching myself.

The three named are based in the USA and all have different back-grounds and different approaches. Here is what one of my clients said once he had worked with one of these for a while:

I have been on this program for over a year and I could easily write a huge amount about this and what it has done for me.

I must stress the "for me" aspect, because traders and their problems are about as diverse as you can get. Everyone's needs are different – it's just like your doctor, he can't cure everything and just because you like your doctor, it is no guarantee that I will.

The program can make substantial improvements to one's trading perfor-mance *and* one's personal life. In my view, they are very much linked. Peo-ple considering using a trading "coach" often consider only trading benefits and not the "life quality" benefits. When considering my comments, bear in mind that trading for me is a hobby and not a full time occupation.

These large "life quality" benefits come about from learning to go within and to increase self-awareness in order to overcome self-sabotage and other negatives.

Each stage of the treatment increases these dual benefits, starting with the Home Study Course followed by the seminars and, in my case, one to one consulting.

It continues to be an enlightening journey of enrichment, self-awareness, quality of life *and* better trading. What is the point of being a good trader but miserable with your quality of life? Is life meant to be just about making or losing money?

The greatest benefit, by far, for me has been my one to one consulting as part of my program, which I have not yet finished. In my experience, the benefits of the program have been so enormous that they are impossible to quantify and, in view of this, it is one of the best and most attractive bargains that I have ever come across.

It must also be realized that the benefits to be gained are directly related to the commitment of the individual and it *does* require an ongoing commit-ment, particularly in order to achieve the levels of self discipline that pro-duce the trading improvements.

My quality of life and my trading results have been transformed.

What more can I say?

(*Parts of this have been slightly edited.*)

It gives me great pleasure to receive a letter like that. I might not be directly responsible but it is a direct result of my work that this individual is reaping these benefits. My philosophy is very simple. Any client of mine is entitled to the very best advice and if that means recommending the services of other people then that is fine by me.

Such responses are typical of those who work with trading coaches (or trading psychologists as they are sometimes called). Here is a comment from one of Adrienne Toghraie's clients:

> I ... want to thank you for your excellent work you did with me through your seminars and most importantly through your personal consulting. Success came unpredictably but consistently into my life after ... going through the multiple other techniques we worked on. I have to admit that I'm happy our lives crossed and that you made a difference in my life. I hope there will be many who will have had the benefit of having worked with you.

If you consider what it would feel like to be consistently profitable in the markets *and* to enjoy an enhanced quality of life, you will see what these clients are talking about. But, as with everything worthwhile in life, it does require work on your side, not just the fees involved. I will come to the fees towards the end of this chapter.

Adrienne Toghraie

But first let me tell you why I decided to use Adrienne Toghraie as my personal "coach." Some years ago I made two major trading decisions. The first was to design and use a trading system (indeed more than one), the second was to stop trading options – although I have now reversed that decision. These two decisions made a big difference to my trading. Once I started to use a system I started to realize where my weaknesses lay. Why was it that the system often made more money than I did? Once I stopped trading options I got a much clearer picture of what I was doing. In fact it was my decision to become "systemized" that led to my decision to stop writing options. I now know precisely where I need to make improvements. They are probably the same areas in which many readers also need to improve.

As an aside I should add that it was what I learnt about my psychology not trading options that allowed me to go back to this form of trading.

First I learnt that I must take fewer trades – I tended to take too many different signals. This can be a particular problem when you hit a successful run, you become over-confident and take everything in sight. Your profits soon disappear when you do this. I have had a number of clients over the years express surprise that they can generate profits but never hold onto them.

Second I needed to let profits run more consistently. Both of these problems come down to discipline, emotional discipline. This is where the coach comes in, he or she finds out what is stopping you from exercising this discipline yourself, gives you methods to follow to help strengthen your own internal discipline, and continues to work *with* you until it works *for* you. That is when the fees charged initially start to be dwarfed in comparison with the money you can make from the markets.

In my own trading I now find that I consistently achieve my goals. I used to take too many signals but Adrienne suggested that I rate each trade before I take it and I find this a useful discipline. I have learnt from experience that you have to let profits run and I find I am now capable of doing so.

Some of those reading this will not understand the need for stops or will not have the discipline to exercise stops. These tend to be two of the biggest problems faced by traders early on in their careers and these can both be very serious problems leaving you open for paralyzing losses. When I say paralyzing, I mean just that. You may find that a loss of a certain size may literally paralyze you, just as a cobra does with its prey. We have all been there, at least I certainly have, and once we have been there we learn why we need stops and also the discipline to use them. But then maybe there is an easier way.

> **You may find that a loss of a certain size may literally paralyze you, just as a cobra does with its prey.**

First steps

However, there is no need to lay down thousands of dollars to start this process working for you. There are a number of first steps you can take which will give you a better idea of how you are going to benefit. One is *Tharp's Home Study Course*, but this is a fairly expensive first step. Books similar to parts of this course are available from your local bookshop at much lower prices. For example books on stress management, overall fitness and diet and neuro-linguistic programming (NLP). I would also suggest that Adrienne's book *The Winning Edge* (how to use psychological power in trading) is a good place to start. The book is reallistically priced and Adrienne also has tapes aimed at specific trading problems, e.g. discipline, motivation, self-confidence.

The last thing I want to do is persuade any reader to purchase something which is going to prove of no benefit. However, it is quite clear that these services can be of enormous benefit. Although this will not apply to everyone, winners go for what they need. If you think there is scope for improvement in your trading then you should do something about it. The first step is to decide that you are going to be a winner, and to go for it!

<u>SUMMARY</u>

- People often use coaching in other activities, notably sport, and readers should consider doing the same with trading.

- My own experience is that a trading coach is invaluable.

- The next step may be to obtain appropriate books and to work on yourself, but ultimately this may be no substitute for the real thing.

Section 2

MARKET TECHNIQUES AND METHODOLOGIES

Chapter 17

SOME POINTS OF PRINCIPLE

The Trading Manual (TM), the first book I wrote, suggested a strategy of writing balanced positions (both short puts and short calls) which did not take into account any perceived future directional move. This is a valid strategy but my experience of trading this strategy over many years suggests that there is a better way to do it. This is simply to take directional positions, i.e. either short puts or short calls (not both) or indeed straight futures.

In the markets a "short" position means to sell the market, a "long" position means to buy the market.

I know that some readers become confused by the expressions "long" and "short," so I will spend a few lines dealing with this. In the markets a "short" position means to sell the market, a "long" positions means to buy the market. Similarly a "short" options position means to sell options. If you are "short" calls you have a short position, i.e. you benefit if the market goes down. If you are "short" puts you benefit if the market goes up, i.e. you are "long." If anyone is still unsure please feel free to take advantage of the **free** consultancy (five minutes) that comes with this book – contact me for details (see page 240).

I now believe that it is better to adopt a directional position for a fairly simple reason – all the best market logic is simple. This is that if you get it right trading is much simpler and more profitable than if you are forced to hedge, which is *always* the case with a balanced option position. Furthermore if you do get it wrong then you can enter a balanced position at a later stage if you so wish. You may lose a little time and you may not get such good prices. However I view these negatives as being a very reasonable price to pay for the advantages offered by trading directionally. In other words this represents a low risk opportunity but I must stress one caveat, and this is that all trading is dependent on price. In 1997 options premium became so attractive that I found an options strategy to work very well. In late 1998 this remained the case but excessive volatility was a negative. So my comments above must be related to what the market is offering at the time.

A few other points flow from this. First, it is often very clear in which direction the trend is moving – every trader must know this. On these occasions we want to be placed with the market, not against it. With a balanced option position we are at least 50 per cent at odds with the market in such a situation. Second, I have said above that you always have to hedge if trading a balanced short options position. However, I am making an undeclared assumption (always beware of such because they can sucker you) when I say that. This assumption is that you are writing close-to-the-money options, i.e. those where the strike price is close to the current market price. Some traders write options well out of the money and in this case hedging is not always going to be necessary. This is good news because when writing well out-of-the-money the premium received is generally insufficient to allow for the costs of hedging, which is why I do not trade in this way.

More general points

At this point I ought to set out a few basic points which I believe affect all trading strategies:

1 There will always be a market logic which will affect any strategy you adopt.
2 If you do not adopt a disciplined strategy then your trading will, at best, be random.
3 If you do adopt a disciplined strategy then you will start to learn a lot about your own psychology and how that impacts on your trading and and you will start to make some real progress.
4 The market logic of writing balanced straddles is that most of the time you will make money. Once every six months or so you will have a tough time. Human psychology is such that position size will tend to increase whilst things go well often resulting in a wipe out when it gets tough.

5   Point 4 is true whether you write close-to-the money or well out-of-the-money options. The problems with well-out-of-the-money options is that the loss could be out of all proportion to the premiums taken.

6   The market will *always* sucker the majority into trading the wrong way against the forthcoming trend.

7   Point 6 can explain why many opt for trading a balanced position. If you are likely to go the wrong way anyway then is it not better to at least get it half right? I believe this logic is false for two reasons. First because the problems with getting it half wrong are far worse than the advantage of getting it half right. Second because there are ways of getting it right often enough so that it is not necessary to get it half wrong all the time.

8   It is often possible to build a good case for the market to move in a certain direction in the medium term, i.e. the next few days. However, trading that signal by selling options does cause a conflict of time frames. Is there any logic in selling an instrument which does not expire for, say, four weeks on a signal which may only give you an advantage over four days?

9   However, selling options is a low risk strategy. The key is to utilize the advantages in line with the logic of your trading style. This is one aspect covered by this book, although it is also designed to help with other strategies.

10 Another key question a trader needs to address is whether it is better to adopt positions all at one go or whether to stagger in.

11 Talking to my broker recently I was again reminded (how could I forget?) how important it is to cut your losses and to let your profits run. We are all more inclined psychologically to do the reverse, when we see a profit we want to grab it and we become fearful that we will lose it, when we see a loss we hope it will reverse. The outcome of these two reactions is that we take profits too early and let losses run. But this is fatal. *The logic is clear.* Losses are going to happen. If your profits are going to outweigh your losses you must let them run.

12 Markets tend to go further than any expect – that is when they don't go as far. Once a market starts to move in any particular direction it is liable to continue. Trading retracements is not therefore that logical a

move. If you do so do ensure that you have a nearby trading reference point. Preferably wait for a low risk opportunity to trade it – but in my experience retracements often don't give such opportunities!

Low risk trading opportunities

One essential feature of successful trading is to develop low risk ideas and the more of these a trader has the better. I use the following main ideas:

1 Selling (Writing) Options.
2 Using Market Profile to sell above value or buy below value. At the same time using "Minus Development" as a trading reference. I may take such opportunities either by selling options, utilizing futures or, very rarely (none in the last four years), by buying options.

> **One essential feature of successful trading is to develop low risk ideas and the more of these a trader has the better.**

3 The concept of patterns aborting is another low risk idea I am working on – see Chapter 22.

All of these concepts will be dealt with in greater detail later on in this book.

A low risk opportunity is one which I define as having the following characteristics:

1 Its potential reward is far greater than the potential of loss.
2 Stop levels are close and are based on sound logic – i.e. Minus Development (MD) (*see* Chapter 18).
3 Ideally it is with the perceived trend not against it.
4 Ideally the entry level is not available for that long a period of time.

Any low risk idea is only such if it is carried out in a low risk environment. This means the following:

1 Do not open a trade immediately before an important news item.
2 Do not open a trade late in the day, especially on a Friday.
3 Do not open a trade at any time when, for whatever reason, risk is enhanced or is liable to become enhanced in the near future.

These factors are illustrated by an occurrence often seen in markets at major peaks or troughs. The market is at an extreme of sorts, either up or down. A news item comes out which would appear to support a continuation of that trend. But instead a strong reversal comes in. The best example of this is perhaps the outbreak of the war in Iraq where a strong rally resulted. The logic is clear. Traders had picked up that a reversal was imminent but the big traders use very strict risk control because that is the only way to become a big trader and to stay that way. So they did not trade until the news was out because at that point there were no further shocks which could upset their trade. It makes sense to watch for this kind of action and to wait for the news to come out first. I realize that this point is covered elsewhere in this book, but it is crucial to an understanding of market action.

Some would argue that if they wait for the news they may miss the best part of the move, and this is quite true. But if you trade ahead of the news you are not taking a low risk opportunity and if that is how you trade you are unlikely to stay in the game for long.

Low risk is essential!

One final word on low risk opportunities. When this phrase was first mentioned to me I thought "A-ha this is the key!" – and it is. But my thoughts were more along the lines that here was the "Holy Grail" and it astounds me that even after 10 years of trading that I should still have this Holy Grail thing inside me. So when a low risk idea was explained to me I was disappointed. "Is that all it is" I said to myself. This is absurd. There is no "Holy Grail" and a low risk opportunity is all you need. Of course it is not that clever, it is just the way you ought to trade if you want to succeed. I do not mean that you should necessarily use those set out in this book – there are many others, but they should follow the guidelines set out above.

Trading tips

These are things which I have learnt about the markets and trading. One of the problems with preparing a list such as this is that many important points I now operate subconsciously. An important point is that what we do well, we do subconsciously, what we do badly we do consciously. Nevertheless I will endeavour to put in as much as I can, although there will be many other lessons to be learnt.

1 Always minimize risk in every way you can.

2 Always trade against some kind of reference point. A reference point is one at which you might decide you are wrong and get out depending on what action is seen at that point. This is particularly true if you are seeking to short a rally, or go long into a decline – wait to see some from of reversal before going in, or use a previous reference point (even then it is better to wait for a reversal). This was a lesson the market reinforced for me. I believe the 15 odd points per contract it cost me was a reasonable tuition fee – and clearly I had something I needed to learn. Perhaps this can be summarized as "know the potential downside whenever you enter a trade."

3 Stay with positions unless you see something which definitely changes your position. I used to have a big problem with this one. I would enter a position based on a solid trading signal – a signal which could be expected to hold good for some time. But I then looked at a five minute bar chart, or something equally short term and I saw something which made me think that the market was going to reverse. I therefore closed my position. Of course sometimes I was right (that good old "random reinforcement" again) but the facts are:

a A short-term signal does not negate a longer term one and to take action on such is absurd.

b The short-term signal in the first place is probably just an illusion.

c Even if some sort of reversal does come in it will not often challenge the longer term signal.

There are, of course, other factors which could influence you to get out of a good position early. But you need to realize that once in a profitable position you start to *fear* a reversal – this fear becomes a powerful motivator to get you out of the market. You need to learn how to deal with this.

4 It is generally best to wait for some form of confirmation before adopting a position, certainly if buying near highs or selling near lows. So if there are only a few points involved wait for them, don't anticipate. This factor is not needed if you have some other form of confirmation at a slightly better level.

5 Whenever you enter a position know at what level you would get out and at what level you would hedge (if appropriate). Make sure you do so.

6 Develop a methodology which suits you (see Chapter 12). Once you have done so keep a careful record of your results and in particular the instances where you did not have sufficient discipline to follow your strategy. Understand why these happened. Use your success rate to build a carefully defined MM system.

7 Know when to break the rules. This of course confuses the issue but trading is an art not a science and sometimes this rule is necessary – but it is generally best ignored.

8 You will learn as you trade with a disciplined approach that the most important factor in your trading is – **you**. Work will be required and I can help in this regard.

9 You have got to learn to let profits run, you do not have a profit until you can move your stop to lock a profit in. Even then overnight gaps (or fast action) might prevent your stop from working.

SUMMARY

- Long and short directional positions are generally better than balanced positions.

- I list some general trading points which I feel will be useful to all traders.

- Low risk trading opportunities are essential.

Chapter 18

MARKET PROFILE AND MINUS DEVELOPMENT

Market Profile

Market Profile (MP) is a method of organizing market information into a format more useful to those who wish to profit from trading markets. Peter Steidlmayer discovered this approach and his genius was simple, he merely brought the ages old statistical tool, the bell curve, to bear on the market. The bell curve has always been something of a magician. It may not turn lead into gold, but does turn chaos into order. Some may say this is a more impressive feat – *see* Figure 18.1.

> **The bell curve may not turn lead into gold, but does turn chaos into order.**

Perhaps death is the best example. Look at a range of individuals and how death strikes may appear fairly random, as do heights, size of feet, etc. But take large numbers and then we find that we have a normal distribution – a bell curve. Few at the extremes and many in the middle. So is often the case with markets.

There is a certain amount of jargon associated with MP which may not be familiar to some traders. I will now seek to explain some of this jargon.

Traders often speak of trending and non-trending markets. Market Profile uses similar, but different, concepts, these being balance and imbalance.

As cash comes in or goes out of the market (from the actions of the longer time frame buyer or seller) this causes sharp price moves – and this action is referred to as "imbalance." The market then has to digest this action and "balance" takes place.

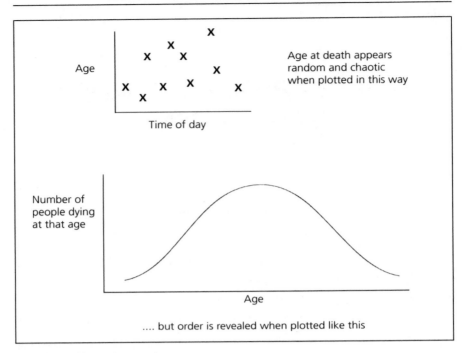

Fig 18.1   Chaos into order

Within the profile for each session similar concepts are development and minus development (MD). I define development as consisting of at least three TPOs (Time Price Opportunities) thick. MD as two or less – see Figure 18.2. TPOs are the building blocks of Market Profile and each price appearing within a 30-minute price segment is a TPO. So MD means that price has spent an hour or less at that price, development occurs when price has spent an hour or more at that level. In a typical profile MD occurs at the extremes and development in the middle – see Figure 18.3. If we were to look at a profile of people's heights we would note that there were not many people who were less than 3 feet, nor many larger than 7 feet. In the market the action within a particular session often forms a "bell curve" which is the classic "Market Profile" form. Where the action is fast there is no development and hence we have the term "Minus Development" ("MD").

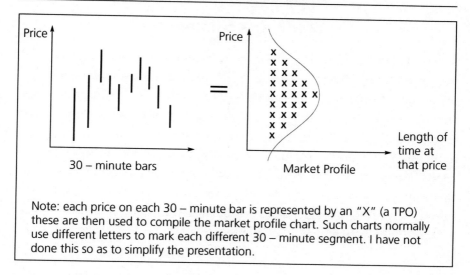

Note: each price on each 30 – minute bar is represented by an "X" (a TPO) these are then used to compile the market profile chart. Such charts normally use different letters to mark each different 30 – minute segment. I have not done this so as to simplify the presentation.

Fig 18.2   The bell curve and TPOs

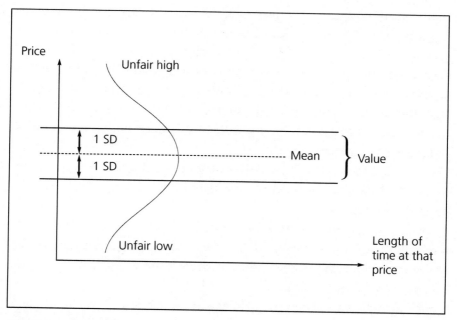

Fig 18.3   The bell curve

Minus Development

MD comes in a variety of forms and is an important concept for "MP" – indeed it is about the only aspect of MP that I use. Most usually it is fast action being formed of no more than two TPOs (see below) whether such action is seen at the extreme of a day's price range (spikes) or whether bell curves form at either end. But it also means gaps (the ultimate minus development) and levels where the market does not go, i.e. a strong resistance level established over a number of time periods. In this way MD is a fairly wide concept and it might be said that MD gives traders the reference against which to measure their trades. Certainly MD provides indications of stop levels.

Value

Perhaps the central feature of MP is the concept of "Value" and this concept is fairly unique in technical analysis to MP – surprisingly so given its importance. When you know where value lies you know that to sell above it or to buy below it gives you a much needed edge. There is, of course, nothing fixed about value and any attempt to be too scientific is bound to fail. Statistically 66 per cent of a range of items falls within one standard deviation (SD) from the mean. This is how MP gauges value, it is the price range one SD either side of the mean within any session, or larger group of sessions.

Earlier I referred to TPOs. Each entry on a MP chart is a TPO (see Figure 18.4), and the reason for the name is obvious, each entry is a Time Price Opportunity.

MP is "fractal" in that it can be applied successfully across a range of different time frames. It seems to be true that the longer the time frame the more reliable the results, and the shorter the time frame the more inconsistency that comes in.

This brings us to one of the primary approaches that can be utilized from this form of analysis – although I am not sure that "MP" should be tainted with this expression. First I must say that it is one of the utmost simplicity – but then this is true of most things which work well. The strategy is simple: look for a signal from the longer time frame (the monthly profiles) and then wait for the shorter term to fall into place. Thus when entering a trade we may look to get an edge on "Value" not only in the short term but also the longer term.

This produces the rationale that unless the trade goes right almost immediately we do not stay with it. But we do not need to – because there are quite enough which do go right.

Fig 18.4   Minus Development

The key to any trading success is taking low risk opportunities. Risk can only be defined if you know what to do if things go wrong. My methodology uses MD to define its trades. I utilize three types of exit approach. First a Money Management stop is placed at a place where I would not expect the market to go – i.e. beyond normative rotational behavior. Second I place a "warning" level either at or beyond MD and if price is "accepted" at that level I get out. The concept of price acceptance may be unfamiliar but essentially if development forms at a level, price is accepted (see Chapter 15). Non-acceptance of price is perhaps an easier concept and a "spike" is an example of this. The third approach is to simply exit if the market does not do as expected. When I enter I am looking for an opportunity available to few traders, if price is subsequently accepted at that level it is a negative and so often I will simply get out.

Once a trade is in profit similar approaches are adopted.

Other concepts

There are a few other concepts which you need to be aware of. The Initial Balance (IB) is the price range during the time taken for the market to find a "fair price," defined as where two-way trading takes place. Usually this takes about an hour but for some markets this may be longer or shorter. Range Extension (RE) is movement beyond this IB – see Figure 18.5. Such movement may either be initiative or responsive depending where value lies in relation to that day's trading. Generally if buyers come in at the low end of value this is termed "responsive," i.e. buyers are responding to the attractive prices. However, if sellers were to come in instead this would be initiative, i.e. sellers initiating further downwards action at unattractive prices. The opposite applies at the high end of value.

The previous day's value, or Value Area (VA), IB, RE, responsive and initiative action, all act as indicators of what is happening in the market and give clues as to what the "longer time frame trader" is doing. Referring back to the start of this piece, the action of the longer time frame trader is what drives directional moves in the market.

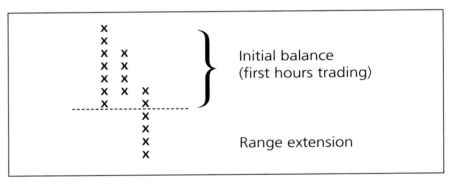

Fig 18.5   Initial balance and range extension

TTT article

The following appeared in *TTT* early in 1998 (there is some duplication but new ideas are often best assimilated if explained more than once in different ways).

For some months we have been working with an institutional trader ("IT") (we set out an interview with him in Chapter 12). This trader has impeccable credentials and has been consistently profitable over the last five years and made significant profits in 1994 when many professionals fared badly. His style of trading is what we might term relaxed. He is looking to catch the intermediate swings and so, on FTSE, he may just trade two or three times a month. But when he does so he is looking to catch significant moves. This is a style of trading I know many readers would wish to emulate and the following is designed to set out the methodology of this trader but also to say a few words about another approach to success in the markets.

As readers to my newsletter will know I am dedicated to helping you make money in the markets, although for novice traders our aim has to be to help reduce losses. We have achieved these aims with some success over the last 10 years, and we can now shed some light on how one extremely successful trader makes his money.

Trading is all about finding and taking "low risk" opportunities. To find these opportunities our IT uses Market Profile ("MP"), which is a way of displaying historic market action to highlight such opportunities.

Before we go into greater detail we must say that MP is a subject about which books have been written. The purpose of this piece is to allow readers to understand the basis of the methodology used and a way of trading using MP. (Appendix 3 sets out recommended books on Market Profile.)

MP is an alternative method of charting historic price action which might therefore be compared to methods such as bar charts, point and figure charts and candlesticks. It differs from these others in that the day is divided into time segments. Initially 30 minute segments were used but this has now been expanded and traders can use whatever segments suit them. Each segment is then plotted against a vertical price scale in the same way as a bar chart except that the price segments are "squeezed" into the vertical axis. For example if the opening segment sees prices between 3100 and 3110 then this will be marked on the chart. If the next segment trades between 3095 and 3105 then the action between 3095 and 3099 inclusive will be marked on the same vertical line as for the first segment and the action between 3100 and 3105 inclusive will be marked alongside the first segment. In this way a profile is built up for each day's action which often resembles a bell curve – see Figures 18.6 and 18.7.

The profile gives further information about market action and in particular can be used to express "value." This is important because, as traders, we want to enter trades offering "low risk" opportunities. A definition of such an opportunity might be to sell above value and to buy below value. Because the profile shows "value" it therefore provides just such opportunities.

Value is calculated as the price action within one standard deviation of the mean on each day and "value" can be expressed as a bid/offer spread. However we need to expand on the expression "mean." MP uses "Time Price Opportunities" (TPOs) and each "tick" on a MP chart is such a TPO. To put this another way, within each time segment there will be a certain price range and each price within this range will form a "tick" and therefore a TPO. It is the mean of all these TPOs which gives rise to the calculation of Value.

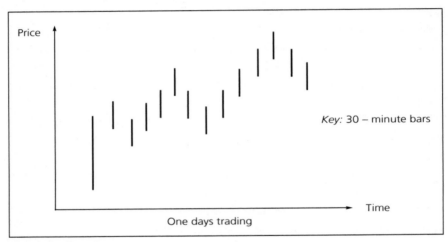

Fig 18.6　Bar chart

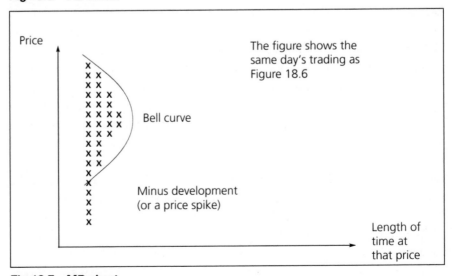

Fig 18.7　MP chart

Another way of putting this, and this can be said to be the underlying principle behind MP, is that Price over Time = Value; or alternatively that Price through Time reveals Value. To understand this statement is not easy, indeed I still have a few problems with it myself, but it does go to the root of this effective technique. In the main it refers to the amount of time for which a particular price is traded during a session.

Once value has been established from the profile of a day's trading it is then important to read the subsequent action. For example if the market quickly falls back and thus rejects the "bid" that is a sign of weakness, but it is not necessarily useful because we want to sell at the "offer" not the "bid" – i.e. we want to sell above value. So an ideal trade would be if the subsequent day we saw a move up to the "offer" price and then a quick rejection of that level with the market falling back.

If we see such action then we have the opportunity of selling "above value" confirmed by the quick rejection of those prices. It is precisely such situations which a good trading system may be designed to capture. Both selling above value, and buying below value.

You will see from this that MP is "neutral" of the market. By this we mean that as you look at a day's profile you do not know whether the following day will provide a low risk buying or selling opportunity. But other techniques used by the IT do give a directional bias. One of these is consensus theory. Our trader has built up a large network of market traders and advisers who regularly feed him information. This allows him to form a view on the consensus and if one becomes clear he is on the alert to go in the other direction. He finds this one of his most reliable indicators. Another is the long-term trend lines which we occasionally publish in *TTT*. When the market is at an extreme, either way, then he knows that an excellent low risk opportunity may be at hand.

So although MP is the motor which drives his methodology there are other techniques which hone it. Also there is a body of Money Management, Risk Control, Discipline, Stress Management, etc. backing up the methodology itself. The interview in Chapter 12 deals with this in a little more detail.

"Chaos makes the new possible, that is its significance"
James Sloman, *Nothing*

Trading tips with Market Profile

In our work we often come across successful traders but when we analyze what they do we find that they just select a few core ideas and use those. As such they may believe that they are "Elliott," "Gann," "Market Profile," or "Wave" specialists, but in fact they are not, they just take a few good ideas and use them to their advantage, and they become expert on these. Incidentally I have never met a pure "Elliott" or "Gann" specialist who is a successful trader – think about it. I believe that Gann and Elliott can be the most misleading techniques in the market today (and it is unclear whether Gann ever made a fortune trading). This is not to knock Gann's work, merely the hype surrounding it.

Nor is my purpose to knock any other forms of analysis, it is to show how MP can be used to make money. The following ideas are useful:

1 The concept of value, as previously discussed, allows beneficial trade location in whatever time frame.
2 The concept of MD is useful for the purposes of trading reference. Some of the strategies set out in Chapter 22 are based entirely around MD.
3 For the purposes of trend following MP has a number of advantages to offer. These can be summarized in the fact that it is only if initiating action against the trend is seen that the trend must be called into question. Further such action which is swiftly rejected is not conclusive – i.e. the initiating action has to be accepted. Thus MP allows a fairly sophisticated trend following approach.

SUMMARY

- The magic of the bell curve turns Chaos into Order.

- Balance and imbalance are Market Profile terms which correspond with non-trending and trending markets.

- Minus development is a key technique of Market Profile which I use every day in my own trading.

- The value area is a central feature of Market Profile although I find I use this less than Minus Development.

- When trading I use primarily three types of exit. First, a Money Management stop which is a fair way away. Second, a closer level, normally beyond Minus Development, where I may exit depending on market action. Third, a "quick exit" if I do not immediately get the action I expect.

- Initial balance and range extension are two additional Market Profile concepts I use.

- Price over time is one of the underlying principles of Market Profile and refers to the amount of time at which the market traded at a particular price within a trading session.

Chapter 19

FUTURES AND OPTIONS

This book is primarily aimed at those looking to trade futures and options, but for the sake of completeness we also want to cover stocks, and our commentary on options will also be suitable for those (misguided souls?) who want to buy options.

Stocks

We will start with stocks, which are the most basic trading vehicle available. The mechanics are simple. You buy the stock and you then benefit from any price appreciation that accrues, and you also receive any dividends appropriate to your period of holding. However, if the price falls away then you suffer a corresponding loss. Gearing can be obtained by borrowing part of the funds to purchase the stocks initially and some brokers also have a similar arrangement. Although most people buy stocks, it is also possible to sell them short. If you do this you are looking to gain because of a fall in the price of that stock. Many people are confused by short selling, wondering how you can sell something before you own it. There is no easy answer to this, you just can, and the position is closed when you then buy it back. So whether you buy or sell short there are always two transactions, a purchase and a sale, you benefit if the sale price is higher than the purchase price, and it doesn't matter which comes first, although the mechanics of the transaction may be a little different. However we must not ignore costs, which are important and which can account for up to 6 per cent on a stock transaction. That means that you have to make 6 per cent just to stand still. It is because of costs like these that it is so difficult to make money in markets because all the profit

> *You have to make 6 per cent just to stand still.*

goes to the security houses which provide the brokerage services. Their profits come from you and me and that is why fewer than 10 per cent of traders make money.

Futures

Futures are not dissimilar to stocks in the way in which they move. If you buy a futures contract you benefit according to the amount by which the futures move ahead, but if they fall you lose correspondingly. However costs are much lower, generally a single tick on the futures. Each FTSE futures contract is currently (October 1998) worth about £52,000 of underlying securities. To calculate this just multiply the current value of the FTSE futures by £10, so it is worth £52,000 with the futures standing at 5200. So if you want to trade one futures contract you have to be prepared to play with around £52,000 worth of stock. Before you can do this the broker insists that you put "margin" down of around £2000/£3000, although often brokers will require more than this to open an account. So you can trade futures giving you an effective gearing ratio of 20: or 30:1. Guess what happens? Private traders go in and do this. But they are scared to death right from the start and "scared money never wins." You can learn how to make money from futures but be sure you know what you are getting into before you start. Of course the costs involved with trading futures are minuscule compared to those of buying and selling stocks themselves.

Readers might like to know why the futures usually trade at a premium to the cash index itself. This is so as to put a purchaser of a futures contract into the equivalent position as a purchaser of the

> **The further out the futures the bigger the premium.**

equivalent value (£52,000 above) of stock. To do this you have to charge the futures buyer a premium in place of the interest which you would assume the purchaser of stock was paying – i.e. you adjust for the cost of the money. The calculation is confused because you have to compensate for the dividends which a purchaser of the stock would receive. If it costs more to hold the stock than it yields, as does FTSE (referred to as a negative-carry market) then you usually get a premium on the futures over the cash. The further out the futures the bigger the premium. That calculation gives you the "fair value" which is the premium, and this will dwindle the closer the futures get to expiry – at expiry the futures equal the value of FTSE itself. However as the futures contract is traded it does not maintain a constant fair value premium over the cash index and what you find in practice is that as the cash rallies the futures put on premium and as FTSE falls back the futures take off premium. This is a simplification, the futures also tend to put on premium as a decline nears support, and takes it off as a rally reaches resistance – i.e. the premium to an extent anticipates the movement of the cash index. These points apply equally well to the S&P.

Options

Now lets have a look at options. Options are one of the most difficult and dangerous investment/trading vehicles available. They also offer some of the best opportunities and strategies.

So how do we sort out the wheat from the chaff and take advantage of the opportunities whilst avoiding the dangers.

Pricing options

First let us analyze how an option is priced by the market, be it a put or a call. Incidentally I am assuming that readers have a basic knowledge of options, know that put options tend to gain value in falling markets, and calls in rising markets, know the meaning of "strike prices," "exercise," "expiry dates," etc. If this is not the case contact me and I will supply explanations of all these terms; alternatively contact your broker.

The main factors affecting the price of an option are:

1 The level of the market as against the strike price of the option.
2 The volatility of the market.
3 The perceived direction (trend) of the market.
4 The length of time remaining before the option expires (reaches its expiry date).

There are other factors, for example interest rates, which affect option prices but these are of secondary importance.

Critical to an understanding of option prices and strategies is an understanding of how the option price is made up of two factors. The first, intrinsic value, is the positive amount by which the option is "in-the-money," i.e. the amount by which the level of the market is in excess (for calls), or below (for puts), the strike price of the option. The second factor and the most difficult and vital, is time value. Time value is simply the difference between the option price and its intrinsic value and represents how much value the market places on the remaining time left in the option. For options which are "out-of-the-money" there is clearly no intrinsic value and as such the option price is entirely time value. Figure 19.1 illustrates how this works.

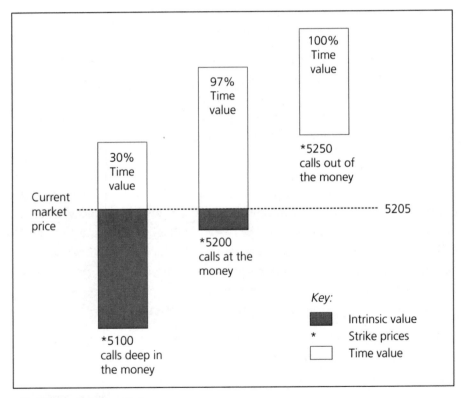

Fig 19.1   Option pricing

A study and understanding of the behavior of time value is necessary if you are to make money in option markets. For example, many traders have often experienced the situation where they purchase an option, the market moves as expected but the option does not increase in value, in fact it may even decline. This is simply because any increase in intrinsic value is negated by a reduction in time value, caused perhaps by a slowing down of the market (loss of volatility), an erosion of the time element (which is, of course, guaranteed), or perhaps because at the time of the original purchase the time value was excessive, and by definition many buy when it is excessive by the principal law of supply and demand; if demand is high then the price is high.

Buy or sell?

This brings us to the question of whether it is better to buy options or to sell (or write) options. The difference between these two alternatives is enormous, and entirely different parameters apply to each. This is only natural as they are the reverse sides of the same coin.

The option buyer has a total limit on his risk, which is limited to the cost of the option, and has the potential for unlimited reward. However, the odds are against a profit being made because of the behavior of time value. Consider seven categories of market action, the

> *The option buyer has a total limit on his risk, which is limited to the cost of the option, and has the potential for unlimited reward.*

first three being a rise in the market slowly, at a medium pace and sharply; the next three being a fall in the market at the same three rates; and the seventh being a flat market. The option buyer will lose money if the market goes against him or is flat and will probably lose money if the market goes in the right direction but slowly. He will possibly break even if the market goes in the right direction at a medium pace and will only make money if it moves in the right direction sharply. So in only one out of seven cases will the buyer make money and in five out of seven he will probably lose – see Figure 19.2. This effect can be minimized by buying options with little time value, for example deep-in-the-money options.

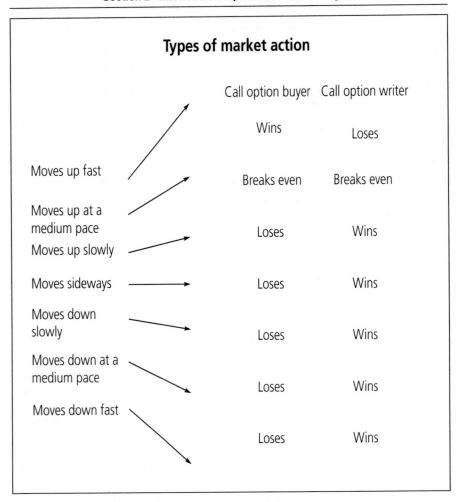

Fig 19.2   Types of market action

Incidentally there is another negative even if the market does move sharply in the right direction. This is that as intrinsic value increases time value decreases. This is because as the intrinsic value builds up so does the buyer's risk, as it is based on the option price, and that increased risk is reflected in a reduction of the time value. However, increased volatility may compensate for this factor.

Now the option writer is in the reverse position. The writer sells the option and receives the option premium, so is immediately sitting pretty as time value diminishes. The writer will make money if the buyer loses and as such will make money in five of the seven categories specified, will break even on one and lose on one. Much better odds. But beware because writers suffer one major problem; this is that the amount of their reward is strictly limited, to the option premium received, whereas the downside risk is unlimited.

The risk/reward profile of buyers and writers lead to the following conclusions:

1 Buyers will normally lose money, but will occasionally do very well.
2 Writers will normally do well, but will occasionally do very badly.
3 The big losers will be option writers caught on the wrong side of a big move. For example there were a number of cases of writers who were bankrupted by the 1987 Crash, and by big moves since.
4 The big winners will be option buyers who catch the big moves.

Now we are ready to look at how to use the two simple option strategies to best advantage.

First a warning, writing naked options is not something which should be undertaken other than in a professional manner and on a full-time basis. There is no other way to handle unlimited risk and I would not recommend such a strategy. Covered writing whereby similar options at a different strike price are purchased is not such a problem. However, the fact that time value is higher as options are further out of the money can result in such a strategy not being worthwhile.

> *Writing naked options is not something which should be undertaken other than in a professional manner and on a full-time basis.*

To the option buyer the essential concern is to minimize the depreciation in time value over the period whilst the option is held. There are five ways of doing this:

1 Avoid buying at times of high volatility.
2 Buy deep-in-the-money options which as such have little time value.
3 Buy options near their expiry date.
4 Avoid the periods during which time value depreciates most quickly, generally about six weeks from expiry until about two weeks from expiry. However, the extreme volatility in 1998 reduced this to two weeks from expiry to expiry itself.

5 Use close time stops, by which we mean that if you expect a move within a certain time period you sell if that does not occur.

Of the above "1" is always advisable; I do not recommend "2" because the risk is too great (although some like this approach); "3" can result in substantial gains but again is very risky as you have to get the market move right and the timing dead right as well; "4" is essential and it is always better to buy longer dated options and trade out of them before the period of heavy depreciation sets in; "5" is difficult because of the problems in forecasting time action as well as price action. On the question of stops, stop loss points should always be used when trading options as with other forms of trading – although they can be difficult to action because the options price can be clearly a bad deal. There are two additional points here. First it is reasonable to use the whole option premium as your stop, i.e. your stop is losing the entire investment in the option – but clearly this has to relate to your capital in accord with your Money Management system. Second, when writing options your stop may not trigger a closing of the position but some form of hedging, either with futures or with other types of option – this point will be covered in greater detail later in this book.

To summarize, our preferred method for buyers is "4" above with occasional use of "3" if a big move is due and it happens to be due at a time when there are appropriate options available.

However, if you are prepared to give up the unlimited potential of your position you can achieve a lower risk profile by writing options at the next strike price further out of the money against your long positions, that is long on options not on the market. This is the reverse of covered option writing but whereas the strategy works against writers it works better for buyers. On FTSE 100 options you can normally achieve a 50 point spread at a cost of about 20 points; on the OEX a spread of 5 points costs around 1.5 points still leaving the potential for a 200 per cent profit. The costs of such spreads will vary from time to time and also will cost less the further out of the money you go.

Unfortunately there is a downside to this form of spread, and indeed to more complex positions in general. This is that the timing of disposals becomes more difficult and often such positions lend themselves to being left to expiry. This is hardly ideal because you are then reliant on the particular market level at expiry and lose the flexibility of choosing your exit point.

As a general rule I believe that it is difficult to make money buying options!

For option writers the strategy is quite the reverse, whereas buyers want to minimize their exposure to time value, writers want to lap it up. The greater the time value the greater the potential for rapid depreciation of that time value and the greater the potential profit. There are three ways of achieving this:

1 Write options at times of high volatility. These often last for short periods of time and very attractive premiums can be obtained. My best ever trade was selling call options on the day of the 1987 Crash.
2 Write options when they have about six weeks to go before expiry when time value begins to depreciate more quickly. In recent months this six week period has fallen to nearer two weeks in the London market on FTSE.
3 Sell out-of-the-money options where the premium is made up entirely of time value, with no intrinsic value.

It is quite possible to achieve all three of the above at once and, of course, such times are the best at which to deal.

Another point of importance is that writers ought to deal when the market is heading in the direction which increases the value of the option in question; for example if the writer is looking to write call options then the market should be heading up. Clearly the trader would expect such a move to be short term and to be followed by a larger move in the opposite direction otherwise he would not be selling that particular option.

The option buyer on the other hand should trade when the market is moving, short term, against the intended position. The reason for this is that options, especially near dated, can be very sensitive to short-term fluctuations and a change in direction can affect prices dramatically.

The purpose of this chapter has been to provide a basic

understanding of the price mechanism affecting options and how they might therefore be traded more profitably. Options provide innumerable trading opportunities and strategies beyond the simple buying and writing mentioned above. To close I set out two such strategies:

1 Writing call options against long stock positions. This is an excellent way to maximize returns from stock holdings. The only risk is that you may miss out on a particularly large move to the upside but in exchange you lock in the premium received on the sale of the calls and you can choose the strike price of those options. That strike price would become the price you would have to accept for the stock if the market moved above the striker and the options were exercised.

2 Writing straddles. The ideal is to write call options at the top of the market, looking at a six to eight week time cycle, and puts at the bottom of the market. However it will be no surprise that this ideal is rarely achieved and one alternative is to write puts and calls at the same striker simultaneously. For example doing this with FTSE options would normally produce between 250 and 300 points for both options but these figures will vary widely depending on the volatility of the market and the time period left to expiry. The same strategy on the OEX would be expected to yield between 20 and 25 points. An alternative is to write puts and calls at different strikers which straddle the market level, this produces less premium but a greater amount of time value. When markets drift in trading bands, which they do fairly frequently, this strategy works beautifully but it is high risk and is not recommended at times when sharp moves can be expected. If following this strategy it is vital to have a hedging strategy in place, for example using futures, for when positions come under pressure.

SUMMARY

- I look at the main trading vehicles available, starting with stocks.

- I discuss futures and how "fair value" is calculated.

- I look at options and explain the major differences in buying and writing options.

- Option buyers should buy when time value is minimized.

- Options writers should write when time value is maximized.

- I end with two strategies, one writing calls options against stock holdings, the other writing straddles and strangles.

Chapter 20

SPIKY ACTION

"Spiky action" sums up my preferred approach to markets. In Chapter 18 I talked about Minus Development (MD) and the best form of MD, in my opinion, is price spikes.

This is a fairly short chapter and I have made it a separate chapter because I think this is vitally important. Everyone who comes to the market needs an edge, something that gives them a chance above average. Spikes do this for two reasons – see Figure 20.1:

1 Spikes tend to show you the direction of the Trading Trend.
2 Spikes allow stops to be placed with *relative* security.

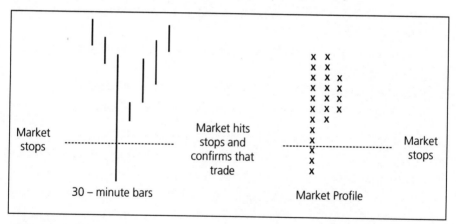

Fig 20.1   A spike

Trading Trend

I define the Trading Trend as the direction of the market in *the timeframe* that you are trading. At any one time a market may have 10 different trends. The very long-term (annual) trend may be **up**, the long-term (monthly) trend may also be **up**. The medium-term (weekly) trend may be **down**, the short-term (daily) trend may be **up**, the shorter term, hourly, 30 minute, five minute and minute trend may be all over the place, and the ticks may be going sideways. Not all of these trends are going to be relevant. In fact I generally just use two trends for my own trading, the Trading Trend (30 minute for my purposes) and the daily trend. I think it is very dangerous to ignore clear signals within your own Trading Trend, but many traders do so.

Types of spike

There are various types of spike – see Figure 20.2:

1 Potential Positive MD – a buying spike which has yet to be followed by development. I define development as three 30 minute bars, either sideways or showing acceleration.
2 Potential Negative MD – a selling spike which has yet to be followed by development.
3 Confirmed Positive MD – a buying spike which has been followed by development.
4 Confirmed Negative MD – a selling spike which has been followed by development.
5 Daily Positive MD – a buying spike left at the end of the day.
6 Daily Negative MD – a selling spike left at the end of the day.

Potential MD is generally weaker than confirmed MD, which in turn is generally weaker than daily MD. But beware of a spike which comes in at or near the close as this will always be a little suspect until we have seen what comes next. Indeed such a spike left at the end of the day may more properly be called potential MD.

Positive MD supports an uptrend and gives a buy signal, depending on your total methodology. Negative MD supports a downtrend and can give a sell signal.

As spikes show determined buying or selling something has to change if they are to be penetrated, this is why I say that a stop placed beyond such a spike has some security.

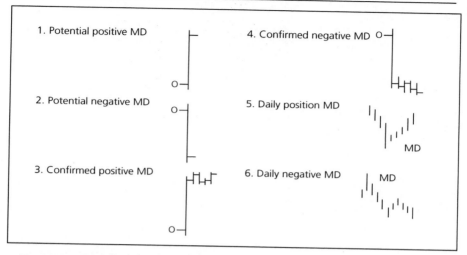

Fig 20.2   Different types of spike

The best form of spike is what I call an "emotional" high or low. These occur when the market is gripped by some exterior force which is driving traders to make emotional decisions, maybe very emotional decisions. In London it can occur when US markets have a particularly strong day and are well up or down as FTSE closes, although a true emotional high or low rarely occurs unless preceded by a decent move in that direction to start with. The fear of what might happen next can drive a market to an obvious extreme at which point we can see either strong buying or selling. Unfortunately this sometimes means a strong opening gap the following day, but then markets are not designed to reward traders, they are designed to maximize trade. Never forget that.

SUMMARY

- Spikes give me an edge for two reasons. First they show the direction of the trend. Second they offer low risk stop points – not *no* risk.

- There are six different types of Minus Development.

- Emotional highs and lows are key levels when the price level itself is clearly driven by strong emotion. The premium, or lack of it, of the Futures against the cash can be a strong clue in this regard.

Chapter 21

AN OPTIONS STRATEGY

Set out in this section are strategies I use in my everyday trading. I have found these strategies useful and profitable. But there are two points I want to make. First I am not recommending that you use similar strategies, similar stop policies, similar methodologies. Chapter 12, "Developing your System/Methodology", in Section 1 makes the point fairly well but it is as well to repeat it. These strategies may not suit your personality, your resources, your trading capital, or your anything. Before using anything put forward by this book ensure that you are going to be able to use it effectively. Second do not assume that because I am outlining these strategies that I am perfection personified when it comes to trading them. The truth is different. I face similar problems to all of us – more of this later on.

The options strategy – principle

I continue to write options despite the problem areas discussed in this book. To reiterate my thoughts on this:

1 Writing options with high time value is demonstrably a "low-risk opportunity." This is so because in most cases options expire valueless and so in "most" cases the strategy will be a winner.

2 However, to trade successfully using this strategy you have to hedge.

3 But hedging means that you will have to take on futures positions at times when that position (the futures hedge) is far from a "low risk opportunity."

4 I now believe that it is far better to trade options directionally – i.e. only writing one leg of a straddle.

5 The rationale behind this is that if it works out trading is more profitable and easier than if writing straddles. Also if you get the direction wrong it should not be that big a problem because you planned for that. If you did not, then stop trading until you learn to consider the downside ahead of the upside.

6 But I tend to find that I always end up with some form of balanced strangle/straddle position. But often at better prices then if I had entered such straight away, and even if that is not the case then generally I have earned some "time." Time is important not only because time value seeps away but because it means there is less time in which you need to hedge.

7 Another "but" is that most signals in the market are short term – or at least you don't know how long term they may be effective for. As such writing options does not tie in with such signals. I often find that I catch a good move only to find that I make nothing from it because it was short term and I am stuck with the options until expiry.

Reading the above you will see that writing options has benefits but it also has disadvantages. You may well ask why I do it, and I do not have an easy answer! It is more difficult trading options because you are tied into the position through some weeks and because you often have to take difficult (high risk) trades.

I have given this question much thought and it has to do with a fear of loss. If I trade futures and lose, say, 40 points then that is quite a substantial loss, even if it only amounts to 2 per cent of capital. But if I have taken £10 000 of options premium then that absorbs the loss and I am not down on the month unless the whole of that premium is eliminated. This gives me a cushion for my trading which makes it far more comfortable. But is this cushion actually serving a useful function beyond making it more comfortable for me? I believe that it is, but I am always analyzing these factors and do not believe that option trading is the only strategy for me. This is why this book is addressed at least equally to futures trading. My previous book, *The Trading Manual*, was entirely about writing options and hedging those positions. There are a good number of distinct futures trading strategies in this book.

The options strategy – operation

Writing the options is fairly easy. Here are the guidelines I use:

1 Write the current month usually (99 per cent of the time). No problem in 1997/1998.

2 Try to get at least 60 to 90 points for each contract written. Again, no problem in 1997/1998.

3 Write at-the-money or near-to-the-money options. You want most of those points to be time value.

4 I tend to write the options in stages. So I may adopt one quarter of my position and then add to that. This seems to work fairly well in practice mainly because I tend to be a little early and this allows some compensation. But this approach is not mandatory.

5 I tend to write one pair of FTSE options (i.e. balanced puts and calls) per £10,000 of trading capital (and one futures contract per £10,000, the same £10,000 as it is a composite position in this instance). I believe that this is about right. Make sure you are comfortable with the number of contracts you are trading and be sure to start small.

6 Use whatever analysis you want (see below) to decide on your directional approach. But it is better to be patient – to wait for the best opportunities. All analysis is flawed and is fairly useless in the absence of market confirmation. I tend to look for market confirmation and place less reliance on analysis.

The market then normally stages some kind of wipe out move and the premiums become attractive again.

7 Before entering any positions ensure that you know what you will do if it goes wrong. Define what you mean by "goes wrong" and outline your precise action in this event.

There are two points I want to add to this list. First, there seems to be a cycle in options prices. They swing from being very attractive to being fairly unattractive. I suspect this has something to do with the number of traders writing options. As the number increases, premiums come down, of course, because there are more sellers. The market then normally stages some kind of wipe out move and the premiums become attractive again.

Secondly I want to set out a list of possible forms of analysis.

1 Any form of trend following system. Write the options that would benefit if the trend continued. For example MACD, Gann Swing Charts, Moving Averages, Market Profile, IOP, etc.

2 Extremes on long term and reliable (if any such thing exists) oscillators.

3 Reliable chart patterns – failed re-tests, flags, triangles, etc.

4 Combinations of techniques

But remember the more certain your analysis – the more likely it is to be certainly wrong!

Options – the hedging strategy

The first thing I will say about hedging is that it is almost always a problem. The reason for this is that you are being forced to enter a position which you would not otherwise enter. Normally when you enter a position everything is as you want it. This is why entry should be so easy, you choose the criteria to suit yourself – it is then just a question of waiting for those criteria to be met. But when hedging it is different, you are forced to trade to protect yourself.

Hedging may be a problem, but we should expect no less. Writing options and taking in all that lovely money (option premium) is so obviously a good deal that there has to be a catch. There is – in fact there are a number of catches. Many get wiped out writing options because they do not hedge, so be warned. Those that do hedge face a lot of problems.

Now I am not the best trader in the world, yet, but my experience has been that it is fairly useless trying to "trade" your hedges. By this I mean that you may as well adopt a straightforward mechanical approach and let it run. The results will be no worse than trying to "trade" hedging and will be a lot simpler to operate.

So first you must analyze your options position, which may become fairly complex, and decide on where you want to hedge.

Incidentally it is best not to allow the position to get too complex as it can then become difficult to know what you should do.

There are two primary and contrary considerations:

1 Should you leave hedging until the latest possible moment, thus giving yourself the greatest chance of not doing it at all, but also reducing the profit potential if you have to.
2 Alternatively should you hedge as early as possible thus maximizing potential profit but engaging in the "hedging" war very early on.

This is another of those cases where there is no free lunch. Whichever you choose has pros and cons. Sometimes you might find that a "low risk" opportunity comes along and that the problem solves itself. Other times you might find that by the time you need to hedge you need to hedge right away.

But to an extent this question is answered by your entry criteria. I have already said that when you enter a position you should decide when to exit or when to cover. So act on those criteria. Write them down and use them.

For my own hedging I use something I call the "Rule of 25" – see Figure 21.1. If we take the typical trading "month" and by this expression I mean the time that elapses between expiries, as one option expires I start to write the next month's and I therefore have four to five weeks to go before they expire. Sometimes if I have a holiday (for example) I may just have two weeks or I might go straight into the subsequent month and have six to seven weeks. However this does not

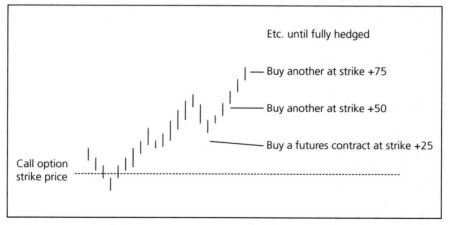

Etc. until fully hedged

— Buy another at strike +75

— Buy another at strike +50

— Buy a futures contract at strike +25

Call option strike price

Fig 21.1   Rule of 25

affect the overall strategy.

The "Rule of 25" is simple. I generally want to hedge the first set of options 25 points (on FTSE) away from their striker. In the case of calls 25 points above the striker, in the case of puts 25 points below the striker. If such options are balanced against the reverse options so that they "cross-over" then 50 points is more appropriate. As with options I prefer to enter hedges in stages. So assume I need four futures contracts to hedge my options I would prefer to enter each contract separately. Following the "Rule of 25" I would enter the four at $X + 25$, $X + 50$, $X + 75$, and $X + 100$, where X is the strike price of the first set of options. By doing this my average entry is $X + 62.5$ which should be fine if I got 50+ points for the options being hedged plus 50+ points for the opposite type of options – i.e. both puts and calls equal 100+.

An alternative to entering single contracts each time is to trade two contracts each time so that all four are in place at $X + 50$.

I may vary the precise entry. I would use established support/resistance areas where possible and I might look to buy pullbacks/sell rallies as possible.

It is vitally important to keep track of when you should hedge – do not "get lost" with other strategies and suddenly find you have forgotten to hedge! (Like I did once!)

To a large extent that is the easy bit. Hedging entry may not be ideal but it is a great deal simpler than deciding when to take off the hedge. *Managing your hedges can be a nightmare.* I have racked my brains trying to solve this problem but I have yet to find a solution. I can, however, make the following points:

1 Do not be greedy. I used to find the temptation to take off a hedge because of all the profit I would make if I got it right. Often I gave into this temptation only to find that I had to re-hedge later on. I think the reason was that I was not taking low risk opportunities when I took off the hedges. I was being driven by greed and thus my thought processes were not as clear. I no longer have these problems.

2 In fact I used to find that I went through a sequence. I would take second rate opportunities to take off hedges, get kicked around by

the market and eventually end up with very little profit potential or indeed a loss. That is when the reversal actually comes in but I am too punch-drunk to take it!

3 It is really all down to trading discipline. Set out your strategy and then stick to it.

Here is my suggestion. Assuming you have written four options contracts you need four futures contracts to hedge. Decide to adopt these in two sets of two. Adopt them as follows:

1 If a low risk opportunity presents itself, use that.
2 If not follow the strategy you decided upon when you first entered the options positions. However you may want to review this strategy every morning and see whether it can be improved upon in the light of subsequent market action.
3 Adopt the first pair of futures contracts on the basis that you will look to enter once the cash market moves 25 points away from the strike price. Enter automatically if the futures market either moves 10 points further or moves 10 points back. Very often you will find that you will get the better price.
4 If the market then moves further out place a stop on the hedge at breakeven – 10, but if you do this you will have to re-hedge if a subsequent reversal comes in.
5 If you see a low risk opportunity which allows the hedge to be taken off take it – but you then have to decide whether it is a long-term or short-term opportunity!

As you can see this is all a bit of a mess and does re-iterate the point that hedging is difficult. The following might help to limit the need for hedging:

1 Take the initial option position with care and only write opposing positions when you have confirmation that something has changed. i.e. *use discipline!*
2 Only trade with four to five weeks to go, no longer; two to three weeks is better when option prices allow.
3 Write the options in stages thus further avoiding the need to hedge.

However, I am also working on a completely opposite approach. This is to put the cart before the horse, as it were. The hedging strategy, by its nature, is a trend-following approach. So initiate the trend-following approach first and then write options to help stay with the position. For example if you are long of the futures at 5000 and you then get very worried around 5220, for whatever reason, sell a few calls (say 50 per cent of the futures) and stay with the futures. The trending strategy will have built in stop levels and if they are hit you still get out, but you have the call premium in hand. You also know that the market has hit your stops, and if these were well chosen, the previous trend is in question. But if the market continues on its way, that is also fine, you may have lost some of your potential profit, but you are still with the trend.

> *You need to know yourself well to deal with these problems and I am not suggesting this strategy for novice traders.*

My final word on options is that I have been trading them for 10 years now. The strategy can get complex and thus falls into the problems discussed in Chapter 11. You need to know yourself well to deal with these problems and I am not suggesting this strategy for novice traders; indeed perish the thought. But those with more experience may find this an answer to their prayers.

SUMMARY

- I outline the principles involved in writing options.

- The operation of this strategy requires careful monitoring and you will be faced with "impossible" decisions quite regularly.

- Hedging is difficult and challenging.

- I use the "Rule of 25" to put on (and take off) my hedging positions. This makes the impossible a little more possible.

- I outline some tips to help if you decide to adopt this strategy.

- Beginners beware:
  Do not enter here!

Chapter 22

A NUMBER OF FUTURES STRATEGIES

There are a number of strategies I use and I set out a list below:

1 Trading gap opens that fail utilizing Minus Development (MD).
2 Trading failed breakthroughs.
3 Trading failed re-tests.
4 Trading breakouts from Square Congestion.
5 Trading with the longer term trend at "key" levels of support or resistance.
6 Elliott Fives.
7 Aborted Patterns.
8 Staying with the "trend" – an impossible dream?
9 Corrective Action.
10 Other "Systemized" Approaches.

As a general rule I will always look to sell above "value" and buy below "value" – this concept is explained in Chapter 18. Of the above 10 concepts, 1, 2, 3, and 5 will always trade at an advantage to value, but the others may not.

Most of the examples in the following chapters are signals which I have personally traded.

Earlier in this book I discussed low risk opportunities and readers should ensure they understand this concept. In that earlier chapter I said that you should treat yourself to only the best signals. But this goes beyond just the simple opening of the position – simple because everything is set up for you at that stage. However we should take the concept of "only the best" beyond the opening stage. I continue to monitor positions in the early stages and if I don't like what I see then I get out. This takes judgment and you have to develop this through experience. By doing this initially you may well worsen your results , but I sometimes find that I now exit even the bad trades with perhaps a point or two in hand – not exactly wonderful but a lot better than a loss!

Finally I would not usually hold any of these positions overnight unless there was a decent profit buffer in hand – i.e. the position is in profit and I judge that profit sufficient to cover any potential reversal overnight. But also I would want to see a good reason to hold overnight and not too many negatives. Often after a good day the FTSE cash may gap open (effectively) but often the futures do not – the futures usually discount the continuation the previous day.

Gap opens – code word: goose

Market action comes in all shapes and sizes. Sometimes it is very easy, other times it is not. It is therefore not possible to give precise rules and it is a case of formulating a strategy. When a market gaps it tends to lead to either a continued move or a reversal. With the FTSE futures, gaps are fairly common but the number of gaps appearing on a daily chart are fairly few which suggests that most gaps do reverse.

> **Market action comes in all shapes and sizes. Sometimes it is very easy, other times it is not.**

Ideally I like to see the following:

1 That the high or low seen in the first hour or so either on the cash or the futures is the high or low for the day.
2 A fairly good move away from the opening level which comes in within the first 90 minutes of trading, preferably sooner.

How quickly I take the trade will depend on the form the action takes, the relevance of the high or low made, and the direction of the trend.

Of these the direction of the trend is the most important. Analysts sometimes make a great fuss about designing techniques to determine the current direction of the trend, but in many cases a five-year-old child would have no difficulty determining the direction of the trend. If you look at a stream there is no difficulty determining the direction in which it flows, and this is most usually the case with the market. Now it is important to be a little objective and at turning points it can be difficult and the same goes when corrections set in. Personally I believe it makes sense to

> *It makes sense to develop a simple trend indicator but that this should be superseded once a trend becomes clear.*

develop a simple trend indicator but that this should be superseded once a trend becomes clear.

So here are a few "simple" trend indicators, the bracketed words relate to downtrends, the main text to uptrends:

1 Are we seeing rising bottoms (falling tops)?
2 Is yesterday's/today's O, H, L, or C higher (lower) then the O, H, L, C X days ago.
3 Is yesterday's close higher (lower) than a Y day moving average.
4 Have I just lost money going short (long)?

Any of these might work well. The trend is often fairly clear and the key is to be objective – too many traders form a view which they then find impossible to abandon. So the purpose of these indicators is really to tell us what we already know but refuse to accept!

Having given you general guidelines I will now give you a specific formula to use although I do recommend that you develop your own. As William Blake said "I must devise a system, otherwise I will be enslaved by another man's." The specific formula is as follows: Use "1" above but where initiating selling (buying) is seen contrary to the uptrend (downtrend) count the trend as "flat" until "1" above functions once again. This will work over any time frame and you need to define your time frame yourself.

So now we can define our trading signal as follows:

1 Determine the trend.
2 Trade with the trend and look to buy (sell) a gap open. Define your own trigger point. For example you might decide to enter as soon as there is any form of rally (decline) off the opening bell on the FTSE cash or futures.
3 The stop is simple in this case – it is X points beyond the opening level. However you might define the opening level as a high or low

in the first X minutes of trading. You may want to use a filter beyond the opening level, say two points or more. However to my mind if the market equals the opening high or low then the rationale behind the trade is much reduced.

4 There might be times when you want to use this approach to trade against the trend. All I will say on this is that you ought only to do this when you have very strong reasons and when the market gives excellent confirmation.

Figure 22.1 shows a typical gap open. The market had just finished a consolidation and this became obvious given the positive opening on 2 August. It was reasonably obvious the previous day given the lack of momentum into the close but the S&P looked suspect. Indeed it fell back quite sharply thus injecting a degree of fear into the market (probably). This chart shows clearly the MD created at the opening and I went long fairly early on, given the overall position. It also showed how the

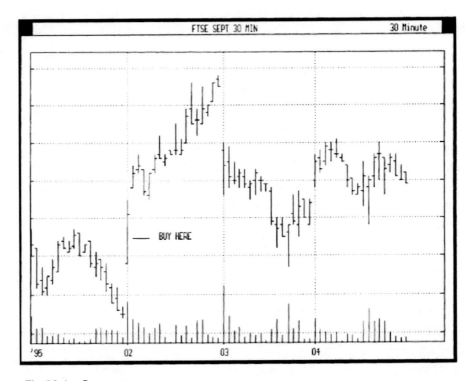

Fig 22.1 Gap open

futures often fall back after such a day. When you get that kind of profit it is best to take at least some of it. It is worth waiting for such moves. As you get more confident with your trading style you will increase position size and a day like that with 20 contracts trading will produce around £10 000.

This book is not about precise trading systems and so how you decide to take profits is a matter for each trader. However there are the following options:

1 If trading with the trend, stay with it until it changes.
2 Close out each day, either at the close or using some form of trailing stop system.

For those who want precise systems I do develop and sell these, always to strictly limited number of traders (never more than 10) (see Chapter 23). Part of the service is to personalize these systems to suit individual traders.

The trend indicators and closing comments are appropriate to all further trading signals outlined in this book.

Failed breakthroughs – code word: goat

Very often a substantial move will follow a failed breakthrough. If you catch such a move then the profits you make will more than cover five times as many losses given that they are always going to be small. At this point I have not done sufficient research to say that trading failed breakthroughs will produce X per cent of winners. This is

> *Very often a substantial move will follow a failed breakthrough.*

something I am working on. But the logic is clear, there is a lot of upside potential, and little downside risk.

The signal I follow is logical. I identify a "key" level. This might be a round number (like 6000, 1150 or 10 000!). It might be an important level of support or resistance, or it might be anything else which I consider significant – but it will be important in one way or another. I generally prefer to see the breakout on the cash index because I consider this more significant – indeed often the futures do not "breakout" and this can be an important part of the signal, often they will have done so in a previous session. Having seen a break which is usually less than 10 points, often just 1 or 2, I then look for the key level to be reclaimed. Once it has been reclaimed the signal is given. Trading this however is not necessarily so simple as it does depend on what exactly happens. For example if a fast reversal comes in I might go with the trade before the key level is reclaimed. If the action is slow then I might look for more confirmation. The stop is beyond the failed break.

One of the key aspects of all low risk entries is that we are looking for important turning points, and other traders are also looking for these. In addition, at such points there should be a preponderance of positions supporting the original move into the failed breakthrough (or whatever else). So the best signals come when we take a trade and a lot of other traders do the same – when we see fast action because the opportunity is too good to miss – when a lot of traders start

The best signals come when we take a trade and a lot of other traders do the same.

to close opposing positions because they recognize the strength. When we don't see such action then the signal is not quite as strong, although it may develop later. It is a mistake to be too particular because you will probably filter out all the signals. So you have to strike a happy medium. Figure 2.2 shows a clear "Goat" above 3539.2. The initial action was pretty positive and we saw a thrust up. However this failed and the market regained the key level. Figure 22.3 shows the same action on the futures. The decline was fairly short lived but it still provided a good short-term profit – often these signals provide a lot more than that.

One important point here: you will always be trading contra-trend so again you must get your timing right – you must have a good reason for thinking that a reversal is coming. But again you have a close stop – the peak of the breakthrough which you perceive as having failed.

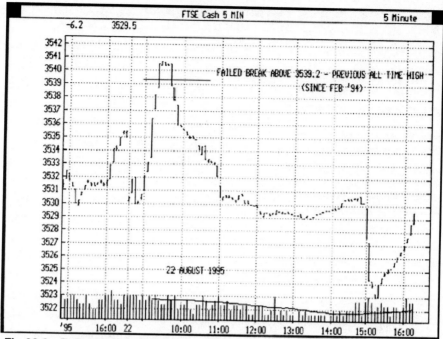

Fig 22.2   Failed breakthrough

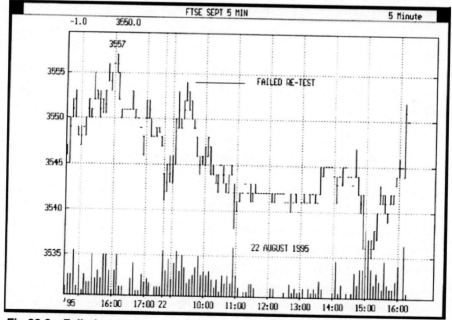

Fig 22.3   Failed re-test

Failed re-tests – code word: snake

We have coded these with the snake because the signal is a little contrary to basic trading logic – i.e. you are selling an uptrend, or buying a downtrend. Also nothing much has changed, so if a market re-tests it might well break through. With a "Goat" something has changed – the market has made new highs (or lows) thus leading to a possible bull (bear) consensus. So the snake is one I do not take so often, which just shows how much my trading has changed because this used to be virtually my only signal. One of the keys to success is to increase the number of available options in as many situations as possible. That way you never get stuck, there is always a strategy to get you back on track.

One of the keys to success is to increase the number of available options in as many situations as possible.

The signal occurs when a market makes a key high or low and then moves to re-test that level. It fails to regain it and instead moves down again. In this case we want to see some fairly fast action and preferably some minus development in place as our trading reference, ie. we want to see that there is evidence that it really is a failure. Stops want to be fairly close for this signal but that should not be a big problem because they will be beyond the high or low being tested – i.e. the stop is operative once the failed re-test ceases to fail. As a general rule I prefer to see these in the shorter term. Chart Figure 22.3 shows a clear "snake" on the futures, corresponding with the "goat" on the cash.

Square congestion – code word: box

This is an idea adapted from a book by Joe Ross (I wonder where he got it from?). For this I use a five-minute bar chart on the futures (note that some of these signals use the cash, some the futures and some either or both) and I look for congestion (sideways action) which is "squared" meaning the highs and the lows of the congestion are made a number of times by the bars within the congestion. Figure 22.4 shows the type of action. The trading signal can come in either direction and is simply a penetration of the range. The stop is ideally at the other side of the congestion which is often fairly close. As with all these low risk ideas look for "squares" which suit you perfectly, be particular, only accept the best, you deserve it! If the stop is too far away then leave it, if you don't want to see the action go back into the range after entry, then get out if that happens. Keep on lowering that risk, go only for the perfect signals. You still won't get it right all the time but the more carefully you refine your trading the better it is likely to get.

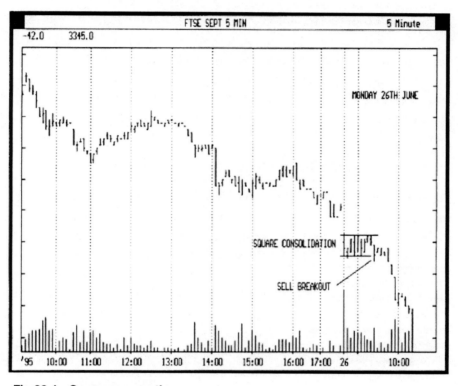

Fig 22.4   Square congestion

Key levels – code word: piano

Market Profile is designed to show what the "longer time frame partic-ipant" ("LTFP") is doing. The logic is clear, short-term traders and locals are not going to move markets because they are not putting anything in or taking anything out. But the LTFP does put money in and take it out.

He causes markets to distribute up and down. One particular point at which we can expect the LTFP to be active is at "Key Levels." This phrase refers to the long-term support and resistance levels plus "round" numbers, plus levels which gain market fame – those which are much talked of, i.e. targets. Having said that, I sometimes use shorter term levels which meet these criteria also, mainly when I need to enter hedging positions on options contracts.

Very often such levels will prompt a reversal of some sort and often it is major. I will normally look for one of the other signals at such a point, a failed gap, a failed breakthrough, or whatever. But often the best trades come from these levels. The decline off the peak at 3405 on FTSE starting on 23 June 1995 is a good example. In essence if I find one of the other signals linked to a "key level" then that enhances the signal and makes the trade more attractive – a better opportunity.

Elliott Fives – code word: illusion

I recently wrote to a subscriber that "I wished I had been introduced to Market Profile when I commenced my trading career rather than the garbage of "Elliott," and I meant it. Elliott's big problem is it pretends to be something it is not. Elliott waffles on about "secrets of the Universe" and other such nonsense, giving the impression that it all has some meaning. Now maybe one day we will all say, so Elliott was right all along, but now it doesn't matter, and it never will as far as any market is

How can any theory which encompasses all types and forms of action have any value? How can you predict what cannot be predictable?

concerned. Markets discount and if somebody finds the "secret" it will be discounted and it won't be a secret or effective any more. Also the logic of Elliott is all wrong. How can any theory which encompasses all types and forms of action have any value? How can you predict what cannot be predictable? The problem is that once you start to associate meaning with any technique which is merely designed to get you into a position, it is that much more difficult to exit when it starts to go wrong – and that is one thing you have got to be able to do. See Appendix 5 for a discussion on "Is Elliott Addictive?"

However the Elliott Five can be a useful signal. I do not intend to dwell on it in detail and if you want to know what it looks like you can either look at Figure 22.5, or read a book on Elliott – which we have included in the proscribed category – because mind pollution can take a while to clear.

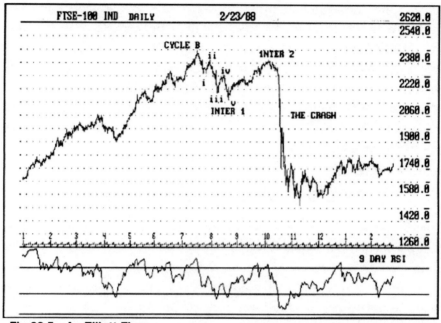

Fig 22.5   An Elliott Five

The signal is fairly clear, if we see a "five" it is an indication that the direction of the five is the way of the trend. It is then a matter of trading to enter the trend. We recommend either one of the low risk opportunities itemized in these pages or entering when the lows of the five have been taken out. The "5" can also be used as a trend reversal signal following the end of the "5" – see also Chapter 24

Aborted patterns – code word: platypus

I have written about these in the newsletters and spoken about them on the hotline for some time. They are probably one of the more important structures which a trader can look for. The reason for this is clear and logical. If there is a pattern developing then a number, maybe a large number, of traders may be following that pattern. Therefore there is already a good reason to look to "fade" that pattern – i.e. trade against it. But before doing so it is better to wait for some sign that the pattern is breaking up. Any patterns can be used for this purpose but Elliott "fives" and "head and shoulders" are two that immediately spring to mind. To an extent a failed breakthrough is an example of such a pattern. When support breaks, it is classic theory that that is a sell signal. If that is aborted and we see a failed break, then we buy. To detail all such patterns, how the pattern may abort, how to trade such and where to place stops, goes beyond the scope of this book but whenever we see a good example we will show a chart in our newsletter. This may also be the subject of a later book.

Trend following – code word: horse

Trend following is tough. How do you stay on a bucking bronco? But that is what a trend is like. It wants to shake off all those traders who are running with it – indeed it has to in order to survive.

We have to accept that all trading has to be a compromise. We are never going to buy all the lows and sell all the highs, we are never going to catch all of a trend. So a good first step is to define a trend. Once we give it a definition we can then use that to catch it – words are indeed cages.

I will use "Market Profile" to define a trend. The definition is that the trend is up in the absence of initiating selling and the trend is down in the absence of initiating buying.

That then defines the stop. We have to see initiating contra-trend action and that has to be *accepted*. To use these techniques properly you need to know where "value" lies. This is a difficult calculation and it is probably best to do it with suitable software. Alternatively you may have to use the range of the previous day to determine whether initiating action of the wrong sort is being seen.

"Acceptance" is a concept discussed in Chapter 15. If the market rejects the break then you want to stay with the trend, if not you ought to get out. As a general rule, you should give the trend the benefit of the doubt as long as possible – if only because it is your friend.

That leaves the entry criterion open. However, we have no particular entry criterion. What we look for is to enter using one of the low risk opportunities

One technique which can be useful is to write options when you feel that the trend is tiring.

already discussed and then, if we have joined the "trend," to stay with it. You might end up with multiple entries. That is fine but you must watch your overall position and not "overtrade."

One technique which can be useful is to write options when you feel that the trend is tiring. So if you are trading an uptrend and are long, say, four futures, then you might write two call options at a point where you might otherwise close some of the futures – not because of evidence of a trend change but because psychologically the market is shaking you loose. You could do this at various stages and it could add a reasonable enhancement to overall profits.

Corrective action

Following on from trends we must deal with corrective action. The job of any correction is to shake out those holding positions with the trend. Corrections use various weapons including time, price, news, and speed. All can help to set up the psychological scene to allow the trend to recommence. It is of course important to differentiate between corrective action and a new trend. Often this is difficult, but we know to expect losses, we know we are not going to get it right all the time. The difficulty of telling whether it is a new trend or not is one of the major problems alongside trying to decide whether we are in sideways or trending action.

Only the most feeble corrections are not going to lead to some action which could be initiating action contrary to the trend we are following. If it is not accepted then we can still stay with the trend, but if we are shaken out we need to re-enter once we have determined, rightly or wrongly, that it is just a correction which has shaken us out.

Figure 2.6 shows a rally following corrective action. In this case the rally aborted negating the signal.

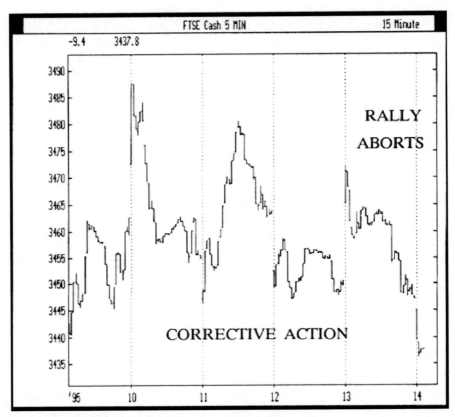

Fig 22.6   Corrective action

Other systemized approaches

These come in all shapes and sizes and are dealt with in more detail in Chapter 23.

SUMMARY

- I outline ten types of futures strategy.
- A gap open occurs when the market sees a gap between the previous close and the subsequent open.
- A failed break occurs when price moves beyond a prior high or low, then reverses.
- A failed re-test occurs when price tests a prior high or low, fails to move beyond it, and then reverses.
- Square congestion is a pattern of broadly horizontal bars. A signal is given when price moves outside the "square".
- Key levels is an important concept referring to market action at previous support or resistance level, or round numbers.
- Elliott Fives are a part of the Elliott Wave theory.
- Trends are difficult to stay with but very rewarding if you can.
- Corrective action is a sign that a previous trend is due to resume.
- Other systemized approaches are dealt with in the next two chapters.

Chapter 23

SYSTEMS

I actively develop systemized approaches to market action which are often developed around some of the low risk ideas set out in this book. So I have developed an intraday system (sold out) which takes multiple positions during the day; another system which trades just once a day – PDS (sold out); a trend following system – Trend-Hunter (a handful of copies left); and the Overnighter which seeks to exploit certain situations occurring between the close one day and the open the next. These systems are incorporated within my own trading rules discussed later in this chapter. A complete list of systems I use in my own trading is included in Chapter 24. The strategies outlined in Chapter 22 form the bases for some of these systems.

I never release a system to more than 10 people and so the price can be relatively high. However, the proof of any pudding is in the eating and the

I never release a system to more than 10 people

same applies to a system – it is only worth what future profits it can bring in. Anyone who buys a system from me does not simply buy a system, but also my commitment to make the system work for him, or alternatively find another route to winning in the markets. This is a fairly major commitment and is one other reason why I always limit the number I sell.

The purchase price of the system also relates to how profitable it is. There is an initial down payment but thereafter payment only takes place out of profits. This requires a certain amount of trust, and as a general rule I prefer to enter into a deal of this nature with someone who I know, such as someone who subscribes to *TTT*. However, this is not a fixed rule.

Stops

I have dealt with stops in some detail already under each category of low risk opportunity listed above and, more fully, in Chapter 15. However, my use of stops has gone through an evolution and that process might be useful to other traders, so here it is.

When I first started trading I didn't know what a stop was. However, I was writing options and if I came under pressure I would limit risk, I thought, by writing opposing options or buying similar options. In this way I went some way towards limiting my exposure and there were certain levels where I would take such action which could be referred to as "stop" levels.

The motto is – if you go out put in place some stops.

I then started to learn about trading (the hard way you can be assured) and I also got involved with futures. At this stage I understood the basics of using a stop. I went through a number of stages. I would use stops on the futures, I would use stops on the cash (my brokers would do this for me), I would use stops a fair way away, I would use very close stops.

I still utilize some of these techniques from time to time, most often when I have to leave the office for some reason or another. There is a cautionary tale on this point. A friend of mine popped out for 10 minutes to get a paper and didn't think he need worry about putting stops in place. He went to cross at the zebra crossing. The first car stopped, the second did not, and the first car was knocked into him. He ended up in hospital and when he was able, found he was well down on his market positions. The motto is – if you go out put in place some stops.

However, there is another point. I now have the discipline to act on mental stops, therefore I do not need to place them in the markets. If you haven't got this discipline then you must place them in the market.

So how do I use stops now? As a general rule I use mental stops, but I also use the concept of acceptance. So I want to see price accepted below my stop level before I get out. Whenever I go out I place simple stops in the market. So the answer to the question is "No, not always." But I *always* look to control my risk and exposure – and that is what you have to do.

One secret to success

This can be looked at as a secret to success or the reason why many fail to make it. The biggest problem I had in my trading was "preconceived ideas" particularly Elliott. I used to see some sort of pattern, became convinced, I think at a subconscious (or partially subconscious) level, of some particular outcome in the market. This then affected all my trading, usually with dire consequences. But this can happen with many techniques. The only answer is to be aware of the problem and then actively discount this illusion. Each trade you do, consider exactly the reasons you are doing it. If illusion creeps in then eliminate it.

All patterns on the market are meaningless – unless confirmed. Once confirmed they remain of some note until negated. Make sure you know when these events occur. Remember *"Trade what you see, not what you think!"* (Joe Ross).

A few additional comments

There should be enough in this book to suit the most feverish trader. If you wanted to you could probably trade two or three times a day following some of these signals. However the key is to be selective. Take only the best – that is a very important concept. Define what you are looking for and then pluck only the ripest fruit. Learn some patience, the more the better.

My own trading

So do I trade these systems? You bet I do! These systems make money and they make it in a low risk and acceptable fashion. Some of the best moves ever develop from some of these signals. They fly in the face of conventional wisdom – at least as I understood it some years ago. All the time you are risking a little to catch a much greater amount.

However, I do not trade them perfectly. There is an excellent book by

Joe Ross called *Trading by the Minute*. In this he makes that key statement "Trade what you see, not what you think!" This is so important. One of my biggest problems

> **You need to distil from this information what you need to develop your own trading plan.**

used to be that I was addicted to Elliott – see Appendix 5. Sometimes an Elliott pattern would form and I found that, contrary to my wishes, I became hooked on the Elliott view. I have found this to be fairly expensive on a number of occasions in the past. But I have now overcome this problem and I now trade what I see, not what I think, thus filtering out views. This process lasts a while because it goes deep and there is always scope for further improvement, but it is critical to reaching your ultimate trading potential.

I realize that I am repeating myself here and there in this book but I think that the more important points ought to be repeated in order to underline their importance.

Also do not think that I am a great trader – I am good, but not great … yet! I have reached a stage where my profits comfortably exceed my losses and it is a direct result of following the principles outlined in this book allied to discipline. Discipline is always a problem. But I have devised trading rules and these allow me enough flexibility so that I can follow them.

My trading rules

This book presents all I know about trading. You may say that it is a little disjointed, that there are not enough conclusions. This would be a fair comment, but to a large extent you must make your own conclusions. That is the essence of trading. It is said that you can lead a horse to water but you cannot make it drink. I have tried to give you all the background data from my experience (as liquid ideas) to allow you to drink, but you need to drink them in yourself. You need to distil from this information what you need to develop your own trading plan.

In this vein, I set out below my trading rules:

Trading rules – August 1998

1 Take only the best opportunities. These are:

a When the trend is clear or (*rarely*) when there is a very strong reversal signal.

and

b There is either opening MD or MD from a key level (failed re-test or failed break) (PDS System).

2 Sell options when "a" is in place so that you are placed with the (perceived) trend.

3 Trade futures when "a" and "b" and *only then.*

4 Hold futures overnight only when good reason to do so and not too many negatives.

5 Consider profit protection/breakeven strategy.

Do – extract charts of all the best opportunities (BO's) and study them.

Stops/hedging

Futures – initially stops beyond MD, try and stay with trends but also try and protect profits. Don't hedge with options until futures are at least 80+ points in profit and then consider carefully whether better to take profits.

Options/hedging

Always leg into positions. Trade directionally initially and then balance if necessary. Do not balance if there are still more than two to three weeks to expiry. Hedge using the rule of 25, or use appropriate low risk opportunities which may present themselves. Do not sell other leg until a clear trend has developed in that direction.

You will see from this that I utilize all of the low risk opportunities in this book and that I have drawn my own conclusions from the discussions about writing options. This book is designed so that you can do the same. You will not choose the same rules as me, I suspect, but you need to choose rules which suit your own trading personality. Formulating your rules should be one of your primary goals once you have read this book.

Risk warning/disclaimer

No true book on trading can be complete without a mention on this. But also the regulatory situation in the UK is such as to require it (well, maybe), however extreme that regulatory situation may be in part. However, such warnings do serve a useful purpose – they serve to bring your/my feet back firmly on the ground. This warning means what it says, it is the real world and before you take any action in the markets it is critical that your thoughts are in the real world – not in the dream world of consistent trading success. I am not trying to sell anything in this book other than reality, and reality is often painful.

In this book I am outlining trading approaches which have proven successful in the market, as outlined above. However, one point must be made clear to traders, even the best systems that have been tested over many years have multi-month drawdown periods. This is a risk in any systemized approach to the market. Money Management and Risk Control are designed to reduce the effect of such circumstances but they cannot eliminate it. So losses will occur, that is certain, and they could be such as to wipe out your trading capital. If the outlined strategies are operated correctly then I would not expect this to happen but I cannot guarantee that it will not, nor can I take any responsibility for any traders' decisions based on such an approach. It is vitally important that you take full responsibility for your own actions in the market – if you cannot then do not trade.

Nothing in this book should be taken as advice to buy or sell any type of future or option, or any other instrument. I am outlining an approach. It is up to you to decide whether such an approach may suit you and any trading decisions you then make are your own.

It doesn't end here

This is not the end, although we are nearing the end of this section – it might instead be the beginning. It is now up to you to decide whether the approaches in this book can help you make money in the markets. As with everything I do I want you to get good value for your hard-earned cash, and so I am happy to discuss this book with you. If you have any points which you would like to clarify then feel free to contact me (see page 240 for contact details). There will be no charge for this but this is *not* intended as a free for all. I will always be happy to discuss and explain anything in this book but there will come a time where such questions will more properly be chargeable as consultancy – see Appendix 1. I will tell you if you reach that point.

Success in trading is all about consistency and to achieve that we must follow the golden rules. These are:

1 Only take the *best* opportunities.
2 Always minimize risk. Taking only low risk opportunities is part of this.
3 Use good Money Management.
4 Have the discipline to follow these rules, especially the first one. It is all too easy to get over-confident and take anything you see. You soon lose your shirt that way. "Only the best is good enough for our trading!" is a good motto to follow.

You can't learn how to do it without doing it.
(attributed to Casanova)

SUMMARY

- I outline my work with systems and my philosophy concerning those who want to buy systems.

- My use of stops has gone through an evolution. Traders must not use mental stops unless they are 100 per cent certain they *will* act on them.

- Preconceived outcomes are a big problem I encountered on my road to success. It is critical to watch the market and to trade what you see (especially if that is contrary to your perceptions) not what you think.

- My own trading has reached a fairly advanced level, but there is scope for improvement – I suspect that will always be the case.

- I itemize my trading rules.

- I set out a risk warning as I think it is essential that traders carefully consider the downside.

Chapter 24

TRADING SYSTEMS AND WHEN TO USE THEM

Trading and living are action, not thought.

John Piper

There are a number of ways to use trading systems as follows:

1 100 per cent mechanically. This is tough and takes discipline, something most traders have problems with, I do myself. I know traders who claim to do well following this approach, but it is not my way.

2 0 per cent mechanically. This covers most traders who try out systems, drop them and go onto the next one. This technique is doomed to failure. You have got to become an expert in your chosen market specialty. One of the first steps is finding your specialty.

> **We never know what the market might present us with at any one time.**

This takes thought and introspection. It is no good acting like a pinball between many different techniques. It is a strange fact that most people who buy systems never use them as intended. About 1 per cent of those who buy systems actually use them.

3 The way I use a system is that I look for the set-up and then use the system that seems most appropriate. As such the set-up is the key, not the system.

Trading systems

Trading systems are all simple entry mechanisms but include all the essential elements of any system which are:

1 Low risk – each system includes a simple exit mechanism which take you out if you are wrong.
2 An obvious trigger point so that the signal is clear.
3 A simple logic as to why this should work.

We never know what the market might present us with at any one time. As such I have developed a number of such systems so that I can enter when I see the appropriate set-up. The systems I use are as follows:

1 V.
2 XXX.
3 Failed Re-test.
4 Failed break.
5 Elliott 5.
6 PDS.
7 Trend-Hunter.
8 The Overnighter.
9 Aborted Patterns.

There is some duplication among these various methods but here is how they work.

V

This is very short term and merely requires the penetration of a prior five-minute bar low or high to give a signal – it gets its name from the five-minute bar, the Roman V is a 5. The stop is the other extreme of the trigger bar. I may use this at the opening if I am expecting fairly determined action, i.e. I have seen a good set-up. At the open the first bar is the trigger bar and if I am looking to go short will do so when the markets make a low below the low of that first bar. I normally trade if it is penetrated by one tick. I may use some form of acceptance for the stop.

XXX

XXX is the same as "V" but using 30 minute bars. Roman XXX = 30.

Failed re-test and failed break

These are set out in Chapter 22 and I have nothing to add to that.

Elliott Five

Chapter 21 also includes comment on Elliott Fives. However, I have decided to revise the Elliott Wave Theory, or at least my interpretation of it. As an alternative I will treat an Elliott Five as an indication of a trend change. I will not assume a corrective move against the direction of the Five. If such a correction is seen then I may look to trade a reversal, but my first impulse will be to fade the Five, once it appears to be over.

PDS

PDS is a system I have sold and have agreed with the purchasers that I would not reveal the precise trading rules. However, the concept behind the system is to look for early determined buying or selling with a view to seeing a spike on the chart which has the potential to become confirmed MD (minus development). However, the actual system rules are secret.

Trend-Hunter

Trend-Hunter is another system I have sold. It is similar to PDS in that it looks for MD, but in this case MD which is confirmed by development. Again precise rules cannot be divulged. However I do have a few T-H systems remaining to be sold. PDS is sold out.

The Overnighter

I used to be very wary of holding overnight but I then realized that this was just one more facet of the fear which the market instills in us all and which we need to overcome if we are to reach our ultimate success. In this respect see Chapter 2 on the Traders' Evolution. One book which helped me was *The Trading Systems Toolkit* by Joe Krutsinger. His logic is simple: if most traders fear holding overnight, as they do, then that is just what successful traders should do. The Overnighter is available for sale.

Aborted patterns

Aborted Patterns are also included in Chapter 21.

How to make a fortune trading futures

If you follow the trading strategy outlined in this book then you will be only trading the best opportunities, getting out quickly if it goes wrong,

> **That mind set is important. You are a winner, not a loser.**

and allowing profits to run. Do that and you have won before you even start. That mind set is important. You are a winner, not a loser. In fact delete the word "loser" from your vocabulary, you will be surprised how important a change this can be – see *Awaken the Giant Within* by Anthony Robbins.

In this section I intend to reveal all the secrets which I have discovered. Some of these you will already know, some of these I have already covered in this book, but part of any secret is realizing its value:

1 When you have caught a good move stay with it. If you find you are focused on exiting, change your focus to adding to the position. As long as the idiot left hemisphere has something to think about it is normally happy.

2 Don't switch tactics, stick with it through thick and thin. Otherwise you will find that as you change so will the market and you will keep missing out. Be patient.

3 The time to sell options is at times of high volatility, especially when everyone else has just been wiped out doing so.

4 You need other people to help you learn this business and to help you realize the value of trading techniques. For example, I would never have realized the value of Market Profile without the help of Pitfox (The code name given to the Institutional Trader who wishes to remain anonymous). See Chapter 12 for an interview with this trader. Incidentally the first thing he asked me to do was read Persig's *Zen and the Art of Motorcycle Maintenance*. If I respect someone's abilities in the market I always do what they ask. I think that is a good rule to follow. In other words you must make yourself an "empty vessel." It is no good going around full of yourself, there is no room for anything else. If nothing else, digest and meditate on this last aspect.

5 But when it comes to trading you must be your own man or woman. Do not follow anyone else, do not listen to anyone else. Go your own way, that is the only way to succeed. This does not mean that you do not use other people's methodologies, or parts of them, but you *must* make them your own. Nothing else will work.

6 Do not fall into the trap of the three time loser. Most traders use a system then drop it when it loses three times in a row. But all systems do this. If you follow this route you will never find success, because you will be constantly changing.

7 You must adjust your focus. Choose the factors you need for your approach and obtain them, using appropriate software, feeds, etc. Then become expert in that approach. You have got to become an expert to win and you are never going to manage it unless you specialize.

8 One of the key lessons to learn is how to handle winning. Because we tend to have less experience of this we have less opportunity to learn. It is not just the discipline loop (where traders are disciplined and make money, they then get complacent and lose, then they pull themselves together again, then get complacent and so it goes, round and round) which is almost facile in comparison, but something that goes to the very core of our being. It is partly that as we learn this business we have to make it alright to lose. Once we start to win we create friction with the structure we have created previously to handle losses. Rules which we know allow us to win start to get broken and it is not clear why. You have to break this pattern.

9 Cut losses.

10 Run profits.

11 Only take the best opportunities.

Absorb all that and you will be a winner – good luck!

SUMMARY

■ I use a trading system when I first see a market set-up.

■ The essential features of any system are low risk, a clear entry signal and a simple logic as to why it should work.

■ I list nine systems I use and explain how most of them work.

■ I conclude with a list of some of the key secrets to success which I have discovered along the way.

Chapter 25

MARKET MYTHS

Indicators and market techniques

I now want to talk about illusion, because illusion is what most trading is based on. This in itself is not the problem, the problem is that many traders give the illusion meaning, when often it is meaningless. The illusion may take the form of Elliott Waves, Gann analysis, RSI divergence, MACD signals, Stochastics, or whatever. The truth is that none of these mean anything. This is not to say that the signals are false, but they will only be correct on a statistical basis, i.e. they have no meaning. They are only as useful as long as the market concurs by its action, once it stops doing so they are worse than useless. In fact to an extent most of these techniques are merely used as an entry mechanism. Entry is the easy part, it doesn't really matter how you enter, it is how you exit that counts. Many traders get hooked on the illusion and lose out because they cannot see that it has become meaningless. The trick is to see the entry mechanism for what it is, just a convenient illusion to get you into the market. Successful traders stay with the trade only so long as it fits their criterion, once that stops they are out. That is the key – entry is largely irrelevant, its only relevance is to give you a trigger for getting in, plus a stop point. Understand that and you are on your way.

To put this another way, traders are obsessed by entry criterion, but most techniques you care to mention are merely entry systems, nothing else, it is when we think of it as something else that problems occur. Elliott and Gann are the worst because they pretend to be something they are not right from the start. The truth is that if you trade with the trend it doesn't really matter where you enter, and if you trade against the trend the same is true. With one form of entry you will win eight times out of ten, with the other you will lose. Can you guess which is which? Actually eight times out of ten is a bit high, but then if you get the trend right maybe not – often though, the perceived trend is not the same as the trend.

News

News in itself has little meaning also. This story illustrates the point.

> There was a poor farmer whose only asset was a fine stallion. One day it ran off. "How awful" cried his neighbours, "what will you do?" The farmer indicated that it was not wonderful but he would see what came next. Next day the stallion returned with two wild mares he had captivated with his obvious charms. "My God how wonderful" said the neighbours. "Maybe" said the farmer. The next day the farmer's son, who did all the work, broke a leg taming the two mares. "How awful" said the neighbours, "will you survive?" "Maybe" said the farmer. Next day the army arrived to enrol young men for the war. "What luck" said the neighbours, "now your son won't be killed on the front line."

The motto of this story is that news is completely irrelevant, it is what follows that is important, and that we can't know. The relevance to trading is that the content is of little import, what matters is how the market perceives the news item and secondly how it reacts to it. So if the market perception is "good" but we see selling, then that gives us a message.

News also creates risk, so you should avoid trading just prior to news items. Low risk positions are available once the news is out of the way.

Zero sum? Don't you believe it!

People say that futures and options trading is a zero sum game. Don't you believe it. It is only zero sum if you can enter and exit for free. You cannot, every time you trade you pay commissions and these make this a big negative sum game. I am ignoring the bid/offer spread which adds an additional cost we must bear unless we always use limit orders, and they have their own problems. This is one of the main reasons why the percentage of losers is so high. All traders are fighting over a negative pot!

Systems

Some traders think that all they need is a system and it will be all right. There is some truth in this as I have explained in this book. However the system has to suit them and very few systems, probably none, are "easy." They all require work and many traders do not really want work. That is one reason why the drop out rate is so high.

SUMMARY

- A few market myths are exploded.

- Indicators and market techniques are mostly illusory.

- News is never really "good" or "bad," it is what comes next that is important.

- Futures and trading options is not a zero sum game, it is a big negative sum game.

- Systems may be an important step forward, but there is more to it than that.

Chapter 26

THE 10-STEP APPROACH TO FUTURES AND OPTIONS TRADING

I have spent over 10 years trading futures and options full time and almost as long working with other traders to help them maximize their potential. Over the years my philosophies both towards trading and towards helping others trade have changed, as you would only expect. In essence my early views were that individual traders had to make the journey themselves and that all I could be was a guide. Now I realize that this is not the best approach. Those starting out towards the goal of unlimited trading success can be given much more than simply guidance, indeed I now believe that they need more than that. Thus I have now developed a simple 10-step process which is applicable not only to those who want to trade futures, but also to those who want to write options, buy options and/or trade stocks. This chapter sets out this 10-step process and serve as an introduction to those who might find the approach useful and to those who would appreciate my help in implementing it.

Step 1: Where am I now?

I have now produced a Psychology and Trading questionnaire (see Appendix 4). Before you can get where you want to go you must decide where you are now, otherwise you will not know what route you need to take. The questionnaire serves two purposes. One is to tell me where you are and allow me to plan a personal programe. The second is more important – it is to make you aware of the manner in which you approach markets and perhaps make clear areas where you will need to work on yourself.

Step 2: Where do I want to go?

If you are going to get somewhere, it is a good idea to know where that place is. As I once said "the man with a plan is many steps ahead of the no-plan man." So we need to define your goals, do you want to manage money, trade for yourself, or what? Maybe you don't really want to trade, if so it is a good idea to find out now. Set out where you want to be in five years' time. Set out the steps you will take to get there. Furthermore you need to know what form of trading interests you. The instruments, the time frame, the type of signal. All these are important aspects and you need to get them right to find your maximum potential. You will probably return to step two throughout the 10-step process, because as you learn more you will be better able to redefine your goals and your preferred methodology.

> *We need to define your goals, do you want to manage money, trade for yourself, or what?*

Step 3: Survival (1)

To survive you have to learn to limit your losses. If you don't survive then you have no chance to learn any more. There are a number of ways of limiting losses and the alternatives depend on the trading vehicle(s) you use and the style of your trading. The following is a range of possibilities:

> *To survive you have to learn to limit your losses.*

1. Use stops that you put in the market.
2. Trade through IG Index (A UK "Betting Shop") where you can place "guaranteed" stops.
3. Buy options, your risk is thus "stopped" at your total investment.
4. Use mental stops.
5. Use stops based on the concept of "acceptance."
6. Use appropriate hedging strategies, as I do when I write options.

For those trading futures often the only real alternative is to uses stops which are put in the market at the same time as you place the trade. This is because most traders have awful problems using stops on any alternative basis. The key to survival is acting when you need to, so you need to use a process that works for you.

Step three is the step that can save you many thousands of pounds. It is the most important lesson you have to learn, because it gives you time to learn the rest of the important stuff.

Step 4: Survival (2)

It's never a mistake to have too much survival in the market. Step four is concerned with Money Management (MM). Again this has to be personalized for each trader and part of the consultancy service is to do just that. I personally find that I like to risk no more than 1 per cent or 2 per cent per trading position, although I risk a little more when writing options because of the nature of the beast. Rule 1 of MM is *never* trade more than one contract until you are consistently profitable. But maybe it should be *never* trade for real until your paper trading is consistently profitable – now wouldn't that have saved some traders a fortune. On FTSE the futures now represent £10 per point. So if you are trading with £10 000 you can risk up to 20 points (=£200 = 2 per cent) and stay within my criteria. Perhaps 20 points is a little tight but it is not too bad, certainly you will often see good trading opportunities with that sort of risk profile. Certainly I could develop a number of precise methodologies risking that or less.

Step 5: Methodologies

This is where we put in place appropriate methodologies. All consultancy clients get precise trading rules for trading failed re-tests and failed breaks. Alternative methodologies can be developed as part of the package. I also have other trading strategies which are available on a no gain, no pay basis. I would mention that this basis only applies to consultancy clients.

The key point of the methodology at this point is that it is clear and precise – that it tells you exactly when you should and should not take a trading position. This is important because you need to know when you are not following the rules. This is the essential purpose of this step. It teaches you about yourself. But this process does not truly start until step seven, so let's wait until we get there.

Another aspect of step five is information. You need to ensure that you receive sufficient information to operate your system. But, conversely, you may find that you are taking in a great deal of information that you do not need. For example if you are operating a purely price driven system you have absolutely no need to read the *Financial Times*, *Wall Street Journal*, or *Investors Chronicle* from cover to cover. You may find that 90 per cent of the information you are taking in is unnecessary. That might free up a lot of time for more constructive use.

> **You need to ensure that you receive sufficient information to operate your system.**

Step 6: Theory

Having got a methodology with which you are happy, the next step is to paper trade it. This is important for a variety of reasons as follows:

1 Something that does not work on paper will not work in the market.
2 Paper trading at least takes discipline. Also it may reveal compulsions you feel to trade for real. Before the time is right such compulsions are inappropriate and it is as well to know you have them, because they will probably be your own worst enemy when you start to trade for real.

> **Having got a methodology with which you are happy, the next step is to paper trade it.**

3 You need to build confidence in your methodology. Back testing is one way, and you need to do this as well, but forward testing is better because you see the signals as they form.
4 You can build confidence in your trading of the methodology by visualizing how you would feel if putting on each trade for real.

So there is a lot to be learnt by paper trading and I believe that this is a key step in the process.

Step 7: Practice

It is now time to trade your methodology (or methodologies) for real. This is no different to paper trading except that you actually put the trades on. The difference is the effect it has on you. This effect need to be minimized and is if:

1 You have an excellent MM system ensuring that your risk per trade is small. Your gearing is true not only of your potential rewards but also of your potential losses and your potential unease. Too highly geared and you may provoke many unwanted psychological problems. Scared money never wins.
2 You have confidence in your trading system. This is one reason why paper trading is important.
3 You have confidence in yourself, especially in your ability to cut losses quickly and efficiently.

Even given these three important aspects many problems can arise once you start to trade for real. This is one more case where the consultancy can help. I have been through this sort of thing many times myself.

Step 8: Fear

Most traders encounter *fear* at some point. This seems an inevitable part of the process and is something all traders have to work through. They do this and reach the oasis of risk-orientation, at which point they stop being fear-orientated. Fear arises normally because of big losses. In many cases the consultancy service will avoid such losses, although not in all cases, because you may be able to lead a horse to water, but you cannot always make it drink. I find that some traders cannot learn other than the hard way. However, fear can also arise through lots of small losses, or it can come from some imagined problem with markets which perhaps happen only rarely. The three steps mentioned under step seven can help. But ultimately it is natural to feel fear in certain situations and you have to realize that many situations carry risk. But that risk is controllable once you know what you are doing. To an extent it is merely a question of becoming comfortable with being a trader.

Step 9: Running profits

Allowing profits to run is the key to making decent profits. It is impossible to make good profits if you only ever take small profits (although this does not apply to all methodologies) because these inevitably are equalled by your small losses (having learnt not to take big losses). It is also impossible to let profits run whilst still *fear* orientated. I have often wondered why letting profits run is so difficult and now realize that it has to do with the first lesson a trader has to learn. It is all too easy to apply the lesson of cutting losses to a small setback when you are in profit. But the result of doing this is that you do not let profits run. To do so you must ride the setbacks which are inevitable.

Step 10: Expertise

The final step is not really step at all – it is a result. You become an expert because you have served your apprenticeship and as a result you become intuitive. This doesn't mean that there is no further scope for improvement, that never ceases to be the case, but you have completed the 10-step process, you have made it, and your consistent gains will prove that.

The consultancy service

The consultancy service means we work together to ensure you make the most of each step. At some stages it will take time to put in place the necessary groundwork, at other stages the process may be quite lengthy, others might pass quickly. The consultancy includes:

1 The Psychology and Trading Questionnaire.
2 Two Precise Trading Methodologies.
3 Access to further methodologies on a "no gain, no pay" basis.
4 An initial consultancy for a three hour session.
5 Full telephone consultancy access for one year.
6 The right to renew the consultancy for a further year if required.

This program is flexible and the actual content for each client will vary. E-mail me if you would like more details (contact details are on page 240)

Thought for the book

Without the risk, without the uncertainty, without the confusion, there would be no profit. So learn to appreciate these factors.

> *Without the negative, we would have no capacity to differentiate the positive. Thus the negative is a necessary precondition to the existence of the positive and our perception of it. So it follows absolutely that one is compelled to take a positive view of the negative, Ipso Facto, the negative is positive due to its positive effect in allowing us to discriminate the positive from the negative. So stop whining, shut up and think positive.*
>
> The Sage, I. Tarius – *Seduction by the Stars.*

SUMMARY

- 10 steps to success:

  1 Where am I now?

  2 Where do I want to go?

  3 Survival (1)

  4 Survival (2)

  5 Methodologies

  6 Theory

  7 Practice

  8 Fear

  9 Running profits

  10 Expertise

Section 3

A CHART TUTORIAL

Chapter 27

LOW RISK TRADING OPPORTUNITIES ON U.S. AND U.K. MARKETS

The purpose of this section is to set out some of the principles explained in the book against actual market action. I have tried not to be too specific in choosing charts as I think it is more important to look at "typical" market action, not that carefully chosen to try and prove a particular point. Too many books cherry pick charts to "prove" something which is in fact highly questionable. Everything happens sometimes in the markets, but illustrating the rarity is not a useful process. In similar vein if we take 100 analysts (or gurus) then statistically one, or more, of them is going to be right at any one time. This is the "lucky monkey syndrome." It is curious that an entire career can be built on this statistical certainty. If you happen to become the lucky monkey for a year or two you can be made for life. I can think of a few examples of analysts who met this criterion and have failed to get much right since – but they remain well known! Very curious.

> **With a selling spike it is stronger if it takes out the prior day's low.**

Figure 27.1 shows an opening spike sell-off, the vertical line denotes the end of the previous day's session. You will also note the two buying spikes shown on the way up. Traders can use these spikes in various ways. As an example let us take the selling spike seen on 5 May. One key aspect of this is that it spiked above the previous day's high and I consider this an important point. A spike which does not do so is not such a strong signal. With a buying spike it is stronger if it takes out the prior day's low. Why should this be so? Because it has probed the obviously placed stops, taken them out, but failed to produce any meaningful selling (in the case of a buying spike), and in fact produced meaningful buying, which created the spike. This means that we have seen a very strong support level, unless something changes. The converse is true with selling spikes as shown on the chart. As it happened that selling spike saw its high at 6105 and was the high seen for the month – something I did not know when I saved this chart to disk. That spike at 6105 was equaled on Tuesday 7 July, but still not exceeded. Figure 27.2 shows the daily chart of the FTSE futures with this particular high highlighted.

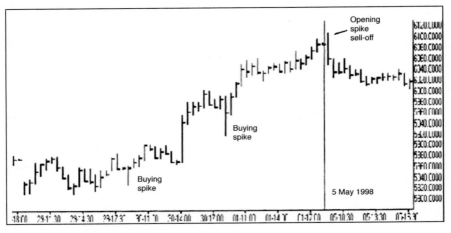

Fig 27.1   FTSE futures 30-minute

The trader has various options when it comes to trading such spikes. He can wait until he has seen a move of X points off the high, X being a variable which the trader can set to his own preference. The smaller X is, the more false signals you will receive, the larger, the more each trade will cost you – remember there are no free lunches in the markets. An alternative would be to wait for the low of the 30-minute bar to be taken out (see the XXX system in Chapter 22). Otherwise you might use five minute bars (see the V system in Chapter 22). Action like this is seen all the time. The signal makes more sense when there are longer term considerations, like a continuing trend or a clear extreme, indicating the trade.

In this case we had a very strong rally into the spike and the chance of the market being a little overbought (meaning there were few buyers left, I am not referring to some meaningless oscillator) was fairly high. We were also at a round number, 6100, and the signal constituted a failed break above this key level. Indeed it encapsulated a number of the principles I have set out in this book. No wonder the following decline has proven fairly robust. Whatever entry mechanism a trader adopted for this move he would come out on top. How much on top would depend on the exit mechanism.

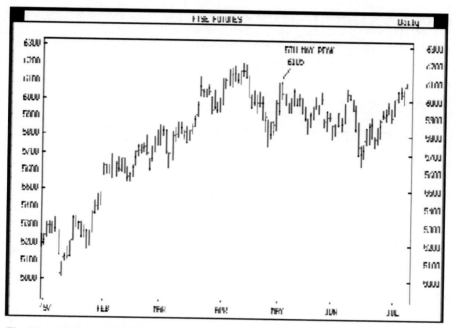

Fig 27.2   FTSE futures daily

Figure 27.3 also shows an initial selling spike but here there are a number of differences. First we had seen a large gap opening to the upside. As markets want to maximize trade they want to close gaps, as there will be trade to be done at all those intervening levels. So we see the selling spike, then a failed re-test and then the market closes the gap. Business as usual. We then see two spikes at the lows. These are buying spikes and suggest a rally, as we then see, not much of one but a rally nevertheless.

As markets want to maximize trade they want to close gaps.

So how did I trade these days. On 7 July I was fairly complacent. I had sold call options at 5800 and 5850 and the futures were now in the high 6090s. I was fully hedged and was looking forward to a healthy profit (15 per cent or more) on expiry in less than two weeks.

When in this position I tend to trade infrequently. I see no reason to fiddle with a position which is looking good. So I ignored the initial selling spike on 7 July as the trend remained clearly up at that time, which suited me well. But once we saw the failed re-test I started to look at the position more carefully. Maybe I should do a full review of markets every night, and indeed I would recommend this, but I prefer to wait until the market tells me that I should take a careful look. That selling spike gave me that message. Figure 27.4 shows the 30-minute action on the cash and you can see how I counted a five wave advance.

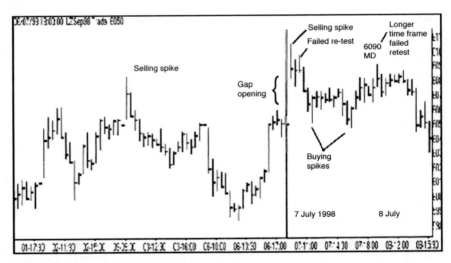

Fig 27.3   FTSE futures 30-minute

OK, this is Elliott and I am addicted to it – see Appendix 5. It isn't even a very good count. But it caused me some concern. There was also a possible interest rate hike due on 9 July. When I am fully hedged I am always conscious that a sharp fall could be very painful. Not only would I lose money on the futures, but also on the put options I had written to balance the calls. So I decided I had better take some action. Just on a partial basis to put me ahead of the game if sharp falls did come in. By this I mean that if I want to take off my hedges, I want to do it in my own time, not because I am forced to do so.

Fig 27.4   FTSE 100–30 minute

One point on mental attitude. I often find myself reluctant to trade because the position is fine as it is and, as my hedging normally loses money, I prefer not to do it unless I have to. But I think this is the wrong attitude, far better to treat such situations as a challenge to relish. Be positive and take the signals as they come in. This makes far more sense. Maybe "Positive Attitude" ought to be another level of the Pyramid? Indeed you might find it useful to personalize your pyramid in this way. There is no need to feel restricted in how you use this model. However, I would not recommend taking any levels away!

Having missed the opening signals, and I do not beat myself up about this sort of thing, it happens all the time, I went short when the subsequent rally turned out to be feeble. Thus I was short into the second buying spike, which I much preferred, otherwise I may have gone short at the lows. I place a lot of stops above highs and below lows when hedging. I often sell the low and buy the high of the day. It's a fame of sorts I suppose! But it doesn't matter, the strategy still works.

I then got out when the closing rally came in. I lost 13 points. That is fine, I had around 700 points in hand with the options strategy and was happy to lose 13 to maintain the position. There is always a little leakage. On FTSE each point is worth £10.

The following day, 8 July – again see Figure 27.3, I was a bit more alert and ready to take positions. When we saw the initial selling spike (marked "MD") I went short at 6080 against the high of the spike at 6090 – another way of putting this is that 6090 was my reference point for the short position, it always pays to use a solid reference point, preferably the tip of a spike. That spike held and I sold a further contract at 6043, having placed a stop below the low of the day. But the decline did not go anywhere and U.S. markets looked good. I closed off one contract at 6042 intending to leave myself 1 short. But then U.S. markets got better and we rallied a bit more so I took profits on the other at 6050. So I made around 30 points and the position was maintained. So a good day's work, I still had 700 points in hand! Chapter 28 details an entire options trading campaign.

Figure 27.5 shows the 30-minute action on the U.K. Gilt market and I have marked the key features on this chart. Numbers 1, 2, and 3 are all failed re-tests. Fairly clear I think. A subsequent bar moves down to test the low, but fails to make it and a rally develops. Of course these signals don't always work although I cannot see any false signals on this chart. Number 4 is an example of spike buying occurring in the course of the day rather than at the open. This merely confirms the uptrend (very short term) in place at that time and is not really a tradeable move due to the speed of the action. I say this because the space between the entry point and the reference point (or stop) can become too big thus making the trade unacceptable in Money Management terms – but then that does depend on your MM system.

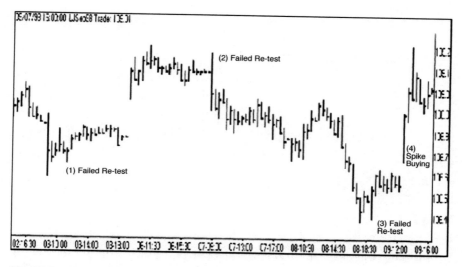

Fig 27.5   UK GILT futures 30-minute

Figure 27.6 shows the 30-minute action on the S&P 500 cash market. This depicts an Elliott count and I prefer to look at cash markets rather than futures for this purpose, about the only time I do so. The reason for this is that futures markets tend to extend moves and I find that the more precise rules often get broken. For example the chart shows the five wave decline off the peak at 1166.09 on 8 July. I was watching this closely because my FTSE option positions were at a delicate point and I felt this five wave decline could be significant. It suggested two things. First that this decline had almost run its course, or maybe had already done so. So I was thinking of buying the S&P or Dow futures at this juncture. Figure 27.7 shows the action I took on the Dow futures. Second that we would see merely a corrective rally, but still eminently playable, to be followed by more downside. So I was watching for a buy signal. The five wave decline itself is of note because it follows the

215

two prime Elliott rules. The first rule is that the third wave is not the shortest, indeed it is the longest, which is normally the case. The second rule is that wave four did not move above the low of wave one – this is often a rule that the futures break as they did on this occasion.

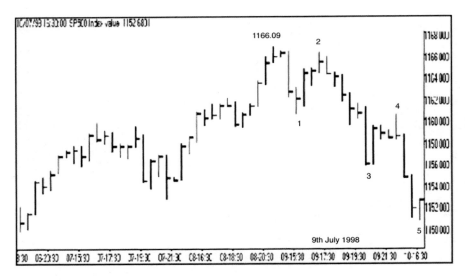

Fig 27.6   S&P 500 cash 30-minute

Readers who are interested in Elliott, something I do not normally recommend, may also like to look at Figure 27.8. You will note a much larger five wave rally starting from the low (a good spike low at that) in late October 1997. Wave five of this larger form was itself subdividing into five waves and this started in late May 1998 (the low marked "4"). It was feasible that the third wave of this final fifth wave had ended and so the five wave decline shown on Figure 27.6 might be signaling that we had the fourth wave coming in before a final, final fifth wave/wave five. Yes, all pretty confusing but potentially useful. Basically it meant that we could be near a major tuning point suggesting an important peak late July/early August to be followed by a sharp pullback. I mention this because it is an important call and

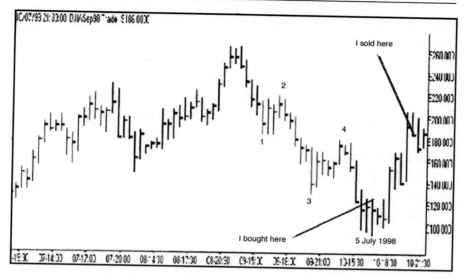

Fig 27.7   The DOW futures 30-minute

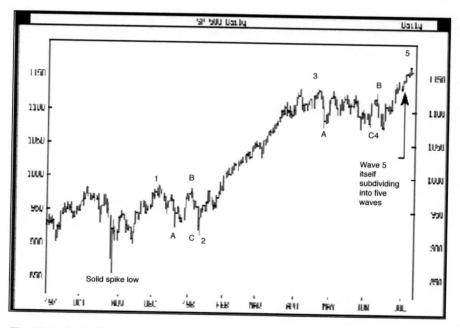

Fig 27.8   S&P 500 daily

although it will be obvious by the time this book is published what has happened, I promise not to cheat! In the event we did see a key peak in July 1998. After all, the signals in this book are ones which only work some of the time, that is one of the important lessons every trader must learn. There is no disgrace in getting it wrong, traders must expect it. Analysts do nothing else, so maybe for them it is different. I don't mean analysts do nothing else but get it wrong, I mean all they do is analyze markets, they do not then trade. Analysis, in my view, is around 5 per cent of the game as far as a trader is concerned.

A trader cannot hope to eliminate risk, he (or she) must learn to live with risk.

An analogy of the trader's experience is that of a tight rope walker. I used to think that a tight rope walker learnt how to balance, but this is not the case. A tight rope walker learns to live with *imbalance*. Similarly a trader cannot hope to eliminate risk, he (or she) must learn to live with risk. In the same way I feel that life itself rarely offers stability and security, we must learn to live with instability and insecurity – and that is how it ought to be!

AN OPTIONS TRADING CAMPAIGN

Chapter 28

A WAR OF ATTRITION

This section outlines a trading campaign I undertook on the London FTSE options and futures market between 3 April and 16 April 1998. In a period of less than two weeks I notched up a 4 per cent gain on the funds I was trading. My benchmark is to make 4 per cent every month which would mean 60 per cent every year. I consider this a very worthwhile target, over a five-year period 60 per cent per annum would mean an absolute gain of over 900 per cent – see Table 28.1.

When I first did this calculation I thought it must be wrong. How can 60 per cent per annum equal 949 per cent over just five years. But it is true. A 100 per cent gain every year equals 3100 per cent over five years. This is the power of compounding. It is the power you give yourself once you become consistent at producing trading profits. I consider writing options one of the best ways of achieving such growth.

Look at the figures in Table 28.1.

It clearly makes a lot of a difference whether you can make over 50 per cent per annum or less than 50 per cent per annum. I am not aware of any other market which can offer this sort of return on a *consistent* basis. It is this potential that makes it worthwhile to become an expert at futures and/or options trading.

It is also the case that these sort of returns can be made without undue risk. Indeed if you get nothing more from this book I hope you do get the message that you have to minimize risk to win at all. Low risk is the only type you want to consider. Anyone who takes high risk positions is going to lose at the end of the day, very possibly lose everything. I have personal experience of this from the early days of my trading and know many others who have been through the same thing.

So let's look at the sort of risks I took to make 4 per cent in less than two weeks. I will use a round figure of £50 000 (equivalent to $80 000 at the time of writing) to illustrate the position. With that sort of money I would limit my trading to just five FTSE options. Each option rates at £10 per point and the margin requirement set by LIFFE is around £2000/£3000 per contract of initial margin. I am therefore trading five contracts with up to five times the amount of margin required by the exchange. But the exchange wants to maximize trade and so margin requirement is set far lower than any prudent trader should consider as realistic. If you are trading at "margin" then you undoubtedly overtrading.

Table 28.1 Growth rates over 10 years

Annual growth rate	10%	30%	60%	100%
Start at	1	1	1	1
After 1 year(s)	1.10	1.30	1.60	2.00
2	1.21	1.69	2.56	4.00
3	1.33	2.20	4.10	8.00
4	1.46	2.86	6.55	16.00
5	1.61	3.71	10.49	32.00
6	1.77	4.83	16.78	64.00
7	1.95	6.27	26.84	128.00
8	2.14	8.16	42.95	256.00
9	2.36	10.60	68.72	512.00
10	2.59	13.79	109.95	1024.00
TOTAL GROWTH				
After 5 years	61%	271%	949%	3100%
After 10 years	159%	1279%	10 895%	102 300%
Value of £10 000				
After 5 years	£16 100	£37 100	£104 900	£320 000
After 10 years	£25 900	£137 900	£1.1m	£10.2m

So let us go through this campaign trade by trade. I call this a war of attrition because as each day goes by the time value in the options diminishes. But my profits can also be worn away as I am forced to hedge. Hedging positions are not "low risk" and usually result in losses. I win when time value erodes more quickly than my profit erodes because of hedging.

Because of these factors I sell options at what I consider to be an optimum time. This is when they have about two weeks left to run under current conditions late in 1998, but this does vary. On FTSE I can

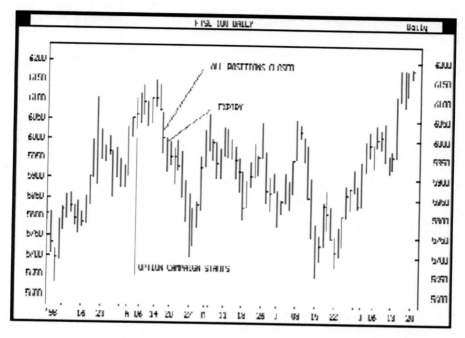

Fig 28.1   FTSE 100 daily

get about 60 to 90 points for an out-of-the-money option at this time, but this does vary with implied volatility, among other things. Figure 28.1 shows the daily action on the FTSE 100 covering the period of this campaign.

Figures 28.2 and 28.3 show the 30-minute action on 3 April 1998 when I opened positions. On the FTSE cash we saw a failed re-test of an earlier high at 6105.8 (20 March 1998) with the high on 3 April coming in at 6105.3. The charts show that we had a fairly good selling response to the attempt to test the previous high. That I took as a sell signal and I duly sold two 6150 calls (over 50 points out of the money) for 61 points. This raises another point which is that I normally leg into positions, adopting one half of position size initially. When the market fell more sharply as the US markets came in badly I sold a further three

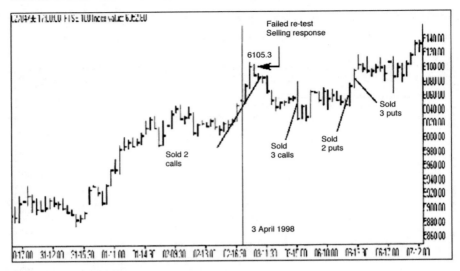

Fig 28.2   FTSE 100 30-minute

contracts of the 6100 calls (again around 50 points out of the money) for 65 points.

At that point I had effectively taken a full short position and had received premium of around £3000 (6 per cent of the £50 000 of trading capital).

If the position had gone 100 per cent right I could have just sat on that and maybe sold some puts if I got a decent buy signal lower down.

But it was not to be. Indeed FTSE rallied into the close and I became concerned that the sell signal was only a short-term affair and that I should balance the position. This I did to a limited extent by selling two 6000 puts at 64 points. Again these were at round 50 points out-of-the-money.

At this time I had had no need to hedge any positions and I had received over £4000. As such I was "covered" down to 5800 and up to 6200. With FTSE closing the day at 6064 I felt very comfortable with the position.

When I say I was "covered" I mean that an expiry between those levels would give me a profit, but an expiry beyond them would give me a loss – however my hedging strategy reduced this risk. As the position stood any expiry between 6000 and 6100 would give me maximum profit of around £4000 (+8 per cent).

Come Monday morning the futures opened with a strong buying spike (see Chapter 20 – Spiky Action) and I felt this was a good enough indication that the trend remained up. I therefore sold three more 6000 puts at 60 – still around 50 points out-of-the-money. You can see from the chart that although the futures saw such a spike, the cash was very quiet.

I now had around £6000 (12 per cent) in hand and the war of attrition could begin. At this point I start to use the rule of 25, meaning that I normally hedge the options when the market goes 25 points above the strike price. The position was a little exasperating because the futures were trading at a premium of over 50 points – which was about right as far as "fair" value was concerned. This creates a problem because I am concerned, on the one hand, to keep as much profit as I can, but on the other to avoid trading as long as possible.

This leads to a certain amount of discretion. I find hedging difficult because very often the trades are "driven." I am undecided what to do at certain points and end up reacting to market action. Often I find myself beating myself up for making "poor" trading decisions, but I think it is far better to congratulate myself for coming out on top. Indeed this is another major point I want to make in this section. Losses are part of this business. Accept that every strategy has its drawbacks (and drawdowns). Learn to accept these and congratulate yourself for the good stuff you do. In the case of hedging I am often faced with impossible decisions. Not surprisingly the result is often losses on the hedging strategy – but profits overall. The key point is to act when you need to, you cannot allow a position to get away from you.

So on 6 April (see Figure 28.3) I saw a strong buying spike on the futures and sold the puts as I mentioned earlier. At that point I had no need to buy the futures as they had not reached the strike price +25. This brings me to another factor which I find a little difficult with this form of trading, which is that it distracts me from directional trading. Given that the options trading allows me to make a good consistent return this does not concern me unduly and this is, again, a factor which I feel I should ignore. Ultimately if you are making money then you should celebrate.

Anyway, the futures continued to move ahead and eventually I went long one contract at 6138. Futures contracts on FTSE are also £10 per point (although prior to this contract they were £25 per point). This is an example of a trade I would not have taken under normal (non-hedging) circumstances. The market peaked a few points higher and then fell back. We saw a low at 6110 followed by a fairly good rally (see the chart) and I then placed a stop below 6110. This duly got taken out and I had lost £300 on the first hedge. Business as usual.

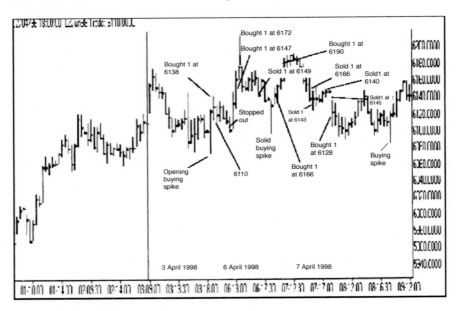

Fig 28.3   FTSE futures 30-minute

My war chest still held £5700 and I only had eight trading sessions to go (the Easter holidays reduced this by two).

The market then thrust ahead again and I bought one at 6147, and a second at 6172. But the market fell back into the close and I bailed out of one of these at 6149. One important point here is that I was looking to go short initially and this gave me a predisposition to short this market. It is better to be neutral.

The following day (7 April) the market opened lower and then thrust ahead once again. I took no action initially and then started to buy more futures as the market advanced. I bought one at 6166 and one more at

6190. The top of the market that day was at 6196 and then we saw another savage pullback. I bailed out of all three contracts at 6166, 6143, and 6140. At that point I had hedged and closed the hedges for a loss of around £1150. A loss of around 20 per cent of the cash I had taken in in two days. There were six more days to go so the attrition had set in with a vengeance, but that also is business as usual. The market always probes in this manner and it is costly when hedging. My trading may not seem brilliant, but it is all part of this strategy. I would rather hedge too often, rather than risk a big loss because the market got way from me.

That day I operated my "Overnighter" trading system and sold one contract at the close at 6145.

The next day (8 April) the market opened lower, but not significantly lower, and we then saw a failed re-test of the earlier low. I took profits at 6128, a few points regained! That day was the sort I hate, where the market seems to want to do something but never does. I bought three more contracts, two at 6117 and one at 6126. I duly sold all of these at 6093, 6101, and 6106. Another £600 down. But still around £4400 left of my original sales, so five days to go and the war chest still fairly well stocked.

The next day (9 April) was the final trading session before the long Easter weekend. The day opened with a strong buying spike and went on to see a significant rally to a high at 6160. I bought one at 6156, only to get stopped out at 6128. The market then rallied again and I bought one at 6124 and then one near the close at 6148 (again using my Overnighter system). So I was long two contracts into the weekend.

The FTSE opened again on Tuesday 14 April and rallied well into a high at 6207. I bought one more contract at 6182. More importantly I was able to close out my five puts for nine points. I always close out my options when they get to around 10 or 15 because they represent a lot of risk and at that price hedging makes no sense. It almost always pays to do so. Such was the case on this occasion.

The 14th was an interesting day (see Figure 28.4). We saw a very clear failed re-test of the high at 6207. This was an excellent sell signal, not only because the market fell back, but because of its form. This illustrates the problem I have when in the middle of an options campaign. To take off my hedges would have prejudiced my profits on the options, although it would have lead to greater profits on directional futures trading. But my primary motivation is as a money manager and my clients look for consistent growth of around 2 or 4 per cent per month. Given this fact I tend to stick with the options strategy except in exceptional circumstances.

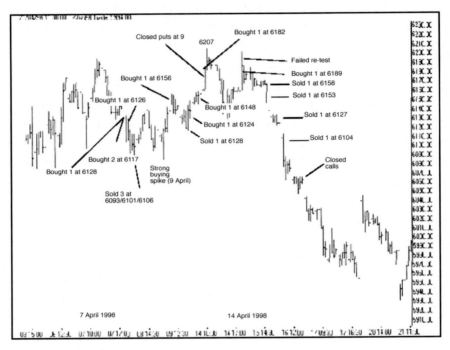

Fig 28.4 FTSE futures 30-minute

So I took no action on this sell signal but did bail out of one contract at 6153 when the market fell further.

The next day the market fell away sharply (thank God I had closed those puts! – thank God I had followed my rules!). I closed out all my futures at 6158 and 6127 on the 15th and at 6104 on the 16th. At that point I had lost around £2800 on the futures, around half of the cash taken.

With the market well down on Thursday 16th I managed to close all my calls. The two 6150s at seven and the three 6100s at 16. I wouldn't normally have paid so much for the 6100s but it was a fairly small price to pay to avoid trading through expiry. Expiry in the UK was particularly volatile at that time. In March the FTSE cash had fluctuated over 200 points (equivalent to a similar move on the Dow) within five minutes as the options expired in March (albeit the March options expiry combined with the expiry of the March futures as well). For comparison purposes Figure 28.5 shows the 30-minute action on the cash during this period.

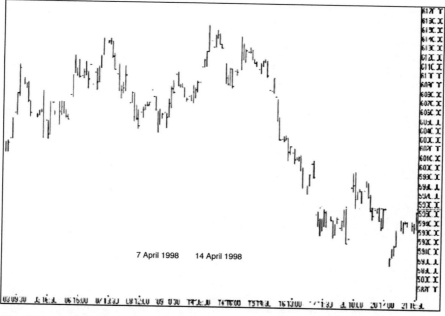

Fig 28.5 FTSE 100 30-minute

It cost me a total of around £1200 to close all the options including commissions. This, plus the £2800 I had lost on the futures meant a total cash outflow of around £4000. Thus I retained a £2000 profit over a two week period – 4 per cent of the £50 000 I was trading, and an excellent result.

EPILOGUE

During August and September 1998 markets worldwide fell back sharply. During this period what struck me were the various attempts to play pin the tail on the donkey, or more precisely to pin the reason on the news – the news in question being that markets had been falling back fast. There were plenty of examples to which the newspapers could point: the Clinton scandal, the Russian *de facto* default, Asia, and any number of other real and imagined problems. But the real reason was, of course, where no one was looking. The real reason was the preceding rallies. These are what led to these falls, everything else is incidental. It is true that some of the other factors may have served as catalysts, but that is all. If markets had not gone too far up in the first place, they would not have been going down so fast. In this regard we must give Greenspan his due, at least he tried to do something about it, but just like King Canute and the tides, it is inevitable that markets will go too high – as they will now go too low at some time in the future. These things are inevitable as long as we use free markets, and what alternative is there?

Markets themselves do not really get a fair hearing. Look at Kuala Lumpar in Malaysia. It is quite comic to visit Kuala Lumpar and see it as a testament to what free markets can achieve, which it is, and realize that Kuala Lumpar was very happy with free markets when they were working its way. But once that changed, everything changed, and the free market is now the "enemy". This is not true, it is merely the tide of human affairs and it will not be bucked. Malaysia, and maybe the whole world, will suffer by their attempts to avoid the natural consequences of their previous success. The whole world, if other countries attempt similar policies. Protectionism has already been tried, and it failed. It merely serves to constrict trade and then there is less for everyone, which is exactly what these measures are trying to avoid in the first place.

In this epilogue my aim is to give a truer understanding of how markets work. I also want to say a few words about my theory of economic black holes, and discuss a few thoughts on free markets.

Perhaps the first point to make is that markets are not fair, as it is from this fact that all else stems. Let's take a simple example of someone buying a car. If you go to the showroom, you see something nice and shiny and you end up paying for it through the nose, in effect. As soon as you walk out the door you are probably down 10 per cent or more. If you were then forced to sell the car in 24 hours you may lose 50 per cent, perhaps more. OK, a car is an item which is sold through clever marketing, etc. and which we expect to lose money on, it is a utility. Financial markets are different, aren't they? Yes, and no. Exactly the same sequence of events detailed above with a car might occur in the markets, indeed many options would immediately give the buyer a 10 per cent loss because of the spread, if not more. Such an option might also expire completely valueless a few day later. Is this fair? Again yes, and no. It is fair if you know what to expect because you will understand what is happening. But it might be viewed as highly unfair by other eyes, especially if you had expected something very different. So it is all a case of perception, but few people are prepared to even accept the possibility that their own perception may be flawed. Some investors may feel that buying a share which was obviously, in hindsight, overvalued, because of high emotion at the time, was a pretty unfair deal. But that is what most investors have been doing for some time now. It is fair because it was the price dictated by the market, it is unfair because it was too far above value. Such an investor may then be emotionally propelled to sell shares into some of the panic selling we saw in September and October and may be left nursing a large loss. Is this fair? In some ways yes, in some ways no.

Markets

Basically markets are a tool and serve a certain purpose but, they do this in a way which is subject to the emotions of crowds. This provides both the problems and the opportunities. If markets are going the "right" way everyone is happy except for those misguided souls who decide to short it because of considerations of value. How misguided can you get? That is not how markets work, which is also the problem.

So, as with everything in life, it is important to understand how it works before you use it. But very few do understand and then they start crying **wolf** when it does not work out as they planned. This is exactly what Malaysia was doing in 1998.

Is there an alternative? I doubt it. How do you stop someone paying too much for something? If they want it, how can you insist the sellers takes less? You cannot. I believe a free market is a necessary condition for freedom generally. Very few people would argue with the concept of freedom itself, but it has the same drawbacks. Freedom gives you the freedom to get into trouble. Markets are one aspect of that.

They are useful and pleasant on the way up, not so nice on the way down. But you can do nothing about it, you cannot have one without the other. The only protection is to understand what is involved and to act accordingly.

The market mechanism is like most of life, not fair. At least not if your mentality is switched onto "loser" mode. Winners don't care, they just go out there and win, regardless! But why do markets move to these extremes, why are investors prepared to pay too much, and sell for too little? The answer is that they are driven to do so, and this goes beyond mere emotion, although this also has its part to play. In simple terms markets generate strong feelings and provide evidence to suggest that those feelings are realistic. So you pay top dollar for a share, only to see the share double, yet again. The decision to pay top dollar in the first place may well have been largely an emotional one, but in hindsight, it was clearly a well thought out decision, wasn't it? Actually, no, it was just luck that you were in the middle of a mania which had not run its course, and such manias make geniuses of the most idiotic. Indeed it is often the most bull headed strategists who win the most.

Economic black holes

This brings me nicely to my theory of economic black holes. The basic point is that as the mania gathers steam you have to make assumptions which, in normal times, would be suicidal. So to compete you end up paying too much for shares, for property, and for other such assets. If you do not pay too much you don't have a business, because you never buy anything. What this means is that when the reversal comes, as is inevitable, you are left high and dry, because the assumptions you made no longer hold true. Thus as a reversal gathers steam more and more of these black holes are revealed and the resulting collapse adds to the problems. Japan is a particularly apt example with all the cross share-holdings adding to the problem because as the market falls the loss on these corporate shareholdings reduces the solvency of the companies involved. Which appear to be most of them.

Bank lending is a similar problem. Once valuations become unrealistic then the loans become suspect. Liabilities can only be repaid in three ways. First they can be actually repaid, the least likely event in this sort of situation. Second the borrower can default as illustrated by the Russian example and this also occurs in bankruptcy. This is very common and is likely to become more so. Third a country can inflate its way out of the problem, thus it need only repay the loan in devalued currency. But this becomes difficult once we get deflation, as we may now have in late 1998 (a newspaper report stated that at one point $2000 billion had been wiped out since the July 1998 peaks), and attempts to inflate away the debt can create the wheelbarrow experience with money becoming virtually worthless, as in Germany in the 1920s and in Russia in 1998. These effects add to the deflation, countries try to protect themselves from the overall depression exasperating the overall effect, and you get a major problem. But in fact it is not strictly a problem, it is a simple reaction to the previous advances, or more precisely to the efforts to maintain the previous advance. Clever financing and exotic marketing become more and more common the more mature a growth cycle becomes. This is because it takes more and more artificial stimulants to keep the action going up, rather like Viagra for the economy. On the way down all those support structures are found wanting, which is a part of my theory of economic black holes. What is very worrying about all this is that you can end up with more and more people fighting for the little that is left. When there is plenty we find that everyone is relatively happy. People share more and there is generally more harmony. Maybe the Irish peace process is one example of this. As things get tighter this changes, maybe dramatically. When I said "fighting" above I meant just that. The Second World War can be said to have had its roots in the hyper inflation seen in Germany in the 1920s. We have sown similar seeds. Russia may head the same way and I can see that war is becoming a very real possibility. This is not a prediction, these things are not inevitable, at least I believe not. But it is a distinct possibility. Whilst I was in Greece recently I was looking at the map of Europe and noticed that Serbia is directly North (my geography is not my strong point). It seems incredible to me that Europe can allow such atrocities so close to its heart. How can someone like Milosevic be allowed to do as he does? Obviously breaching a country's sovereignity is a major issue and there are many practical problems, but if we do not cut such things at their root they can grow and infect much bigger areas. My knowledge of military matters is almost as bad as my geography and I would have thought that Serbia and Russia do not pose major problems right now, at least to Western Europe, but this might change. The war against Iraq in 1991 was won quite easily but it was still a major effort against one fairly minor country. It would be quite another matter if a number of such countries chose to combine their efforts. The current economic situation is of the sort which can generate such things.

LTCM

To get back to markets, I said earlier that emotion was part of it, but being "driven" was more than that. Given the extent of the rallies seen maybe we should steal a phrase from rock band **Pantera** and say "far beyond driven!" I think the LTCM debacle provides a fairly good example as this illustrates a number of good points. This fund was clearly overtrading. Gearing at 50:1 is just asking for trouble and was bound to cause a problem at some time. It is just amazing that such supposed experts can make such elementary mistakes. I also understand from Richard von Goetzen (who writes the *Stock Market Stalker* and who manages his own hedge fund) that the computer models at LTCM used only bull market data. Fine, but any idiot might have thought that some bear market data might have provided some perspective. So LTCM was just one more accident waiting to happen. But what I find more interesting is the reaction of the banks involved. First LTCM repaid substantial amounts of capital in 1997 and the banks complained violently, apparently, although those that got repaid now feel a lot happier. LTCM repaid this money because markets were getting more difficult and they had trouble placing it in the markets (maybe they should have reduced their gearing?). Then they hit problems not forecast by their computer models. A report from **AllWeather** suggests that such strategies as used by LTCM worked as long as non-correlations stayed within three standard deviations, August experienced five + standard deviations. But if you use limited data in the first place then your deviations are going to be artificially small to start with.

Anyway, LTCM had a problem and the banks which were investors had a problem. Did they provide more cash or did they cut their losses? This is where the driven bit comes in. Some of these banks could not really afford the losses involved. Maybe some of the bank's employees concerned would have lost their jobs if such losses had been written off at that point. Some of the individuals concerned at the banks apparently also has personal investments at LTCM which gave them a clear vested interest in giving further bank support. All these factors served to "drive" the banks to run their losses and "average" by throwing more good money after bad. The $3.5 billion bail out was another stage in the same process. Similar factors serve to drive rational investors to buy stocks at silly prices, I often buy the market to hedge naked call options, these trades are similarly driven, albeit in my case they are strictly short term.

The effect of this additional cash is that it allows LTCM to leave these positions in place and maybe they will get better, maybe they will recover all that is currently lost. But it may get worse. That is the gamble the banks are taking, and if they could not afford to absorb the initial smaller loss, how can they afford to risk that greater loss?

Conclusion

I hope this Epilogue has given readers an insight into how I believe markets work. To support these beliefs all I can say is that markets have yet to throw anything at me which does not fit in with these beliefs. I do not know whether U.K. equity markets will now move to new all time highs, but I do know that an extreme high will be seen at some point and there will then be plenty of bad news as markets start to move towards the extreme low which will follow that extreme high. But the real impetus will be the way in which the market works and if you understand that then you will have taken a few steps forward.

APPENDICES

Appendix 1

FOLLOW-UP SERVICES

I set up *The Technical Trader (TTT)* in the late 1980s because when I started trading there was very little help available in the UK. The only sources were from brokers and that is a little akin to putting your head in the lion's mouth. It is important to realize that a broker is better rewarded the more business you do. This is not necessarily in your best interests. I am not suggesting that all, or even many, brokers will want you to overtrade, but it is best to avoid such conflicts of interest.

My basic philosophy was, and still is, "What can I do which is going to help traders?"

I set out below a list of the services available:

- **Newsletters:** *TTT* is issued twice each month. These newsletters do not just provide analysis of the markets covered (FTSE, S&P, Nikkei, US Bonds, Gold, and the UK Gilt) but, more importantly, I discuss many trading factors, particularly psychology and strategy, throughout each newsletter - and I consider this the real value. In this way I draw subscribers' attention to trading points which they may not have considered previously. These "signposts" can be invaluable and you only need to find one useful to pay for the year's subscription. As Harry Schultz might say, *TTT* is really *free*, because it should pay for itself. *TTT* costs £245 ($375) per annum, with a special deal in the first year (see page 240).

- **Hotline:** Markets move too fast for even a weekly newsletter to keep in touch. Therefore I have a hotline on **09067 360360** (charged at £1 per minute at all times). This is probably my most valuable service to traders, giving up to the minute trading tips and advice. This also concentrates on trading tactics and general trading knowledge. Updates are at 10.00 am, and 3.00 pm, plus our special weekend report at midday on Saturday. This service is available by phone in the UK or by fax and e-mail worldwide.

- **Seminars:** The seminars I consider essential. A day's seminar enables me to outline my philosophy of trading in detail and also establish a dialog with subscribers. So far I have developed two seminars: "The Traders' Workshop" which is designed as an introductory session covering trading, technical analysis and the all important psychology which is so critical to trading success. My new seminar "Low Risk Trading" covers the material in this book.

- **Consultancy:** A number of clients want more immediate contact to help out on markets and trading. This service is designed for them - see Chapter 26. As with systems I strictly limit the number of clients I work with – I cannot afford to let this work interfere with my trading.

- **Technical analysis software:** In partnership with Technical Advantage Software we have developed the packages "Gann Analyst" and "TT1." "TT2" combines the two. I use this software myself for my everyday trading – what more can I say? We can also help with real time software offering Market Profile.

- **Systems:** I have developed a number of trading systems, based upon the principles in this book, and I also work with individual traders to develop systems which suit them. Contact me (see below) if you would like to discuss systems or trading generally.

- **Money Management Services:** For details of account management please contact Andrew Woodward at Berkeley Futures Ltd, a firm regulated by the SFA. Berkeley Futures are at 18 Saville Row, London, W1S 3PW. Tel: (0)20 7758 4777; fax: (0)20 7287 5292; email: john@john-piper.com.

To contact the author:

By e-mail – john@john-piper.com

Special deal on *TTT* newsletter:
Contact me and quote this page number for a 60 per cent discount on the first year's subscription (first time subscribers only).

Appendix 2

THE TROUBLED TRADER

by Tony Plummer, MSTA

I am including this article by Tony Plummer as it sets out the working of the "triune" brain clearly. It also sets out the various likely responses and biases that individuals of each type may be prone to. This information can prove invaluable to any trader. I am much indebted to Tony Plummer and to his publishers, Kogan Page, for permission to use this piece. The article was published in the *IFTA Journal* a few years ago and was then incorporated, in an amended form, in Tony's excellent book *Forecasting Financial Markets*.

Making money by trading the financial markets is very difficult. This is a fundamental truth. Unfortunately, it is almost impossible to convey this truth from one person to another; it can only be realized by the very act of trading. Accordingly, very few people enter the trading arena with their eyes fully open to the personal psychological and financial risks. Many will quickly leave after small, but scary, losses. But many more will struggle on with a mediocre performance in the hope that circumstances will ultimately improve.

The corollary of this is that truly great traders are very rare. Jack Schwager's books on "Markets Wizards" would not otherwise be best sellers. But what is it that separates such traders from the rest of us? How can some traders make regular – and large – profits, while others are unable to string two successive winning trades together? Much has been written on this subject in recent years, and it transpires that there is really only one area in which a person can be sufficiently different to be a successful trader – *this is in the area of personal psychology*. Success depends on two complimentary qualities: the ability to maintain emotional equilibrium in the face of trading losses; and the ability to make decisions independently of other people.

The theory behind this conclusion is basically very simple. Trading is a risky and stressful occupation. Very powerful negative emotions are triggered either by losses or by missed profits. These emotions, especially when experienced over a prolonged period of time, ultimately cause traders to herd together psychologically for protection. Traders as a group therefore increasingly do the same things at the same time and, inevitably, the majority are on the wrong foot when a reversal materializes.

The problem is that the sub-conscious mind all too easily dominates our behaviour. Insofar as it is possible to measure these things, scientists think that as much as 97% of our mental activity occurs in the sub-conscious part of our mind. This is a staggering figure and deserves more attention. What it basically implies is that a great deal of our current behaviour consists of learnt responses to familiar stimuli.

It follows from that, that our learning experience – particularly as children – is critical to our behaviour. It is, however, extraordinarily difficult to amend our learnt patterns of behaviour in later life. Why is this? In part it appears to lie with the structure of the brain itself. In the early 1970s, the American neuropyhsiologist Paul Maclean introduced the concept of a "triune", or three-part, brain into scientific thinking. He argued that the brain has three layers, which have evolved over millions of years. The inner part of the brain – the brain stem – derives from our reptile heritage and deals with instincts and biological drives. The next part – the limbic system – derives from our basic mammal heritage and involves emotional activity. The outer part – the neo-cortex – is the part which makes us specifically "human". It involves fundamental reflective thought processes and imagination.

The processes of the brain are, of course, very complex; but each part of the brain is physically and chemically independent of the other parts to quite a large degree. The specific *human* problem therefore appears to be that the neo-cortex is not properly integrated with the other two parts. It is simply too recent an addition. The neo-cortex uses its powers of imagination to help create an internal picture of the external world. This picture – *which is totally accepted by the psyche as being "reality"* – then triggers certain emotions. These, in turn, generate automatic responses. The neo-cortex does not necessarily step in either to control these responses or to re-imagine the external world.

In trying to explain this problem, recent research has focused on the front part of the neo-cortex. This area deals with true individuality –

especially *self-awareness* and with *compassion* for other human beings. In general terms, this area of the brain appears to be underused. It has been found that, where people are receptive to instructions given by others – that is, where they are hypnotized, or are following the direct instructions of an accepted authority figure, or are immersed in the belief system of a crowd – then mental energy patterns remain at the rear of the brain, and therefore in the sub-conscious.

In other words, true individuality is much rarer than we believe. This is a harsh conclusion to reach and the philosophical conclusions are immense: first, it confirms that non-rational mechanical behaviour (notably aggression) is more likely to occur in the context of a crowd than in a situation where a person is acting independently. Secondly, and as a corollary, it indicates that the use of logical thought processes is not a sufficient condition for the avoidance of non-rational behaviour, since the logic may be built around a base of strong, group engendered emotion.

Now, the human mind is obviously dependent on *all* three parts of the triune brain. The mind is a *self-organizing* system, just like any other part of Nature; and it simultaneously controls, co-ordinates and consists of all three functions of instinct, emotions and thought. Consequently, the psychology of each individual is constructed from a blend of these three areas. However, there is strong evidence that there are very subtle differences in the way that we each use the three areas. Hence some of us are regarded as being motivated by *instincts*, some motivated by *emotions*, and some are seen as being *thoughtful*. It is this bias which helps to determine the essential nature of the *personality* which we present to the world. This does not imply any value judgements, it just means that each of us has a bias towards one particular type of motivational energy.

While we certainly prefer to use one aspect of our three psychological areas more than the other two parts, we also prefer to use one aspect *much less*. The third part then lies in between. This line of argument suggests that we might be able to define *character traits* in terms of combinations of the basic psychological areas. Let us give numbers to each part – namely, 1 for instinct, 2 for emotions and 3 for thinking.

There is, however, a slight complexity to be introduced here. This is that the instinctive dimension to our drives can be characterized according to whether they are impulsive or non-impulsive (passive). There is a tendency for some people's instincts to be very *active*, while for others instincts are decidedly *passive*. So the instinctive dimension of the sub-conscious may be denoted as either 1a for the active instinct or 1p for the passive instinct.

It is mathematically true that there are twelve possible combinations of three characteristics, where 1a and 1p cannot be used together. As it happens, however, in those cases where the instincts are *least* used, it doesn't matter whether they are theoretically "active" or "passive". Furthermore the combinations 1p-2-3 and 1p-3-2 turn out to be so similar, because of the dampening effect of passive instincts, that they can be treated as identical. This leaves us with nine combinations and these are shown on Table 1.

Table 1   Basic character types

Type	Character	Bias
1a-2-3	Impulsive–Emotional	Overdeveloped relating
1p-2-3/		
1p-3-2	Passive	Out of touch with relating
1a-3-2	Impulsive–Thoughtful	Underdeveloped relating
2-1a-3	Emotional–Impulsive	Overdeveloped feeling
2-1p-3	Emotional–Passive	Out of touch with feeling
2-3-1p	Emotional–Thoughtful	Underdeveloped feeling
3-2-1a	Thoughtful-Emotional	Underdeveloped doing
3-1p-2	Thoughtful–Active	Out of touch with doing
3-1a-2	Thoughtful–Impulsive	Overdeveloped doing

Each combination type is associated with a specific character type; and each character type is, in turn, associated with a specific type of behavioural bias. In the area of instinct, the bias involves attitudes towards *relationships* with the external world; in the area of emotions, the bias relates to *feelings*; while in the area of thinking, the bias involves the attitude to *doing*.

So let us just take a quick look at what these combinations might be saying about someone. What does it *mean* to be a 1a-2-3 type person, or a 3-2-1a type person? Let us look first at the instinctive people – those that are "gut" orientated.

The 1a-2-3 people – driven by an impulsive/emotional character structure – have their ability to relate to the external world *overdeveloped*. In a sense, they sub-consciously believe that they are bigger than the world. They are likely to be self-confident and forceful; and they organize and lead. However, they may be aggressive, sometimes to the point of being destructive.

The 1p-2-3 and 1p-3-2 – the truly passive people – tend to be *out of touch* with relating to their environment. Such people tend to be peaceable and reassuring. However, they can also be slothful and neglectful.

The 1a-3-2 people – with an impulsive/thoughtful character – are going to have their ability to relate to the world *underdeveloped*. They sub-consciously see themselves as being *smaller* than their environment. They are therefore likely to be principled and orderly, responding to the world's requirements. They can, however, be perfectionist and punitive towards others.

We now move on to the "heart" – orientated people, who are defined by the way that their feelings are engaged.

The 2-1a-3 people – being emotional/impulsive – will have their feelings *overdeveloped*. Positive emotions will be emphasized and negative emotions will be suppressed. They will, therefore, be caring and generous, but also potentially possessive and manipulative.

The 2-1p-3 people – the emotional/passive people – are *out of touch* with feeling. They tend to be self-assured and competitive. Under pressure they can be self-centered and hostile.

The 2-3-1p people – emotional/thoughtful – will paradoxically have their feelings *underdeveloped*. They will not express their true feelings directly, but use other mediums to express themselves. Such people actually tend to be artistic, creative and intuitive. However, they can also be introverted and depressive.

Finally we come to the thinkers – that is those that are "head"-orientated and who are defined by their attitude to doing things.

The 3-2-1a people – with a thoughtful/emotional – have an *underdeveloped* ability to do things. This is not surprising because of the neglect of the instinctive functions. Such people tend to be perceptive and analytical in their approach to the world. But they also tend to be somewhat eccentric and (under pressure) paranoid.

The 3-1p-2 people – being thoughtful/passive – are *out of touch* with doing. Individuals with this structure are dutiful and likable. They are also dependent on others and, under pressure, may be self-destructive.

And the 3-1a-2 people – who are thoughtful/impulsive – have a tendency to rush about because their ability to do things is *overdeveloped*. They are usually accomplished in the sense of having a broad experience of life. But they can also be very impulsive and somewhat excessive.

It is, of course, always dangerous to try and place precise labels on human nature. However each person could – with a little introspection – determine his or her own particular character type. The reward would be some astounding insights into personal motivations.

The point is that *every* one of us falls into one of the nine categories shown in Table 1. It is as if, when we are born, a metal ball-bearing is set running around the edge of a nine numbered roulette wheel within our psyches. At some stage – usually before the age of five – we confront our separateness in the world and the ball drops into a specific indentation. For the rest of our lives, that indentation will be the centre around which our personality structure constellates. Specifically, we will always be on the look-out for particular threats and will always have a distinct *automatic* response when those threats are spotted. Furthermore, this response is usually *hidden* from us. If we are aware of it at all, we see it as a strength, because it has served us so well in the past. In fact, however, it is our central weakness.

It is absolutely essential to understand this in the context of financial markets. Our automatic responses ensure that we each have a *vulnerable spot* within our psyches. Financial markets will seek out that vulnerable spot with unerring accuracy and will accordingly trigger automatic and self-defeating behaviours. I wish to define these weak spots and the likely response mechanisms. Then we have taken a big step towards doing something about them.

So, the next step is to observe that each character structure has two aspects, as it were: a defensive *focus of attention*; and a likely *mode of response* to a perceived threat. In other words, each character trait is like a coordinated radar and weapon response system: it surveys the environment for threat and then responds with an automatic reaction if a threat is identified. These two extra dimensions to the character traits are shown in Table 2.

Table 2 Character type and basic motivations

Type	Character	Focus of attention	Response to threat
1a-2-3	Impulsive–Emotional		
1p-2-3/		Protection of	Aggression or
1p-3-2	Passive	Personal space	withdrawal
1a-3-2	Impulsive-Thoughtful		
2-1a-3	Emotional–Impulsive		
2-1p-3	Emotional–Passive	Protection of	Hostility
2-3-1p	Emotional–Thoughtful	ego	or deception
3-2-1a	Thoughtful–Emotional		
3-1p-2	Thoughtful-Active	Minimalisation	Anxiety
3-1a-2	Thoughtful–Impulsive	of fear	or pretence

A perceived threat can, of course, mean a number of things. It can, for example, mean a direct physical threat. Here, however, I am referring to a *psychological* threat. Such a threat is experienced when there is a divergence between expectations (derived from sub-conscious beliefs) and actual outcomes. In financial markets, therefore, a threat is perceived if expectations of profit are not met. The resultant stress will likely energize one of a number of possible automatic, or *compulsive*, responses.

Let me therefore take you onto the next stage by indicating the details of these compulsions. There is a different one associated with each type of character structure. Each compulsion makes us avoid a particular condition or situation. Hence, for example, a 1a-2-3 person will try to avoid being seen as weak; while a 3-1a-2 individual will avoid physical or psychological pain. Table 3 sets out the various avoidance compulsions for each combination.

I would suggest readers consider how useful (or more correctly how negative) the various avoidance compulsions are in terms of market action and trading. An understanding of this process can go a long way to improve your trading.

· What *strategies* will each individual adopt when faced with a situation which energizes their avoidance compulsion? What happens when an individual feels threatened?

Table 3 Character type and basic avoidance compulsion

Type	Character	Avoids
1a-2-3 1p-2-3/	Impulsive–Emotional	Being seen to be weak
1p-3-2	Passive	Getting involved in conflict
1a-3-2	Impulsive–Thoughtful	Any form of imperfection
2-1a-3	Emotional–Impulsive	Not being liked/recognised/loved
2-1p-3	Emotional–Passive	Failing in chosen tasks
2-3-1p	Emotional–Thoughtful	Being just an ordinary person
3-2-1a	Thoughtful–Emotional	Having insufficient data about life
3-1p-2	Thoughtful–Active	Making any wrong decisions
3-1a-2	Thoughtful–Impulsive	Physical or psychological pain

For each type of person, there is a specific *initial* defensive response once a perceived threat is encountered. These responses are shown in Table 4. In very general terms, the instinct-orientated people will have to deal with actual or potential emergence of *anger*; the feeling-orientated people will have to deal with an impact on their *self-esteem*; and the thought-orientated people will have to cope with the actual or potential emergence of *fear*. Hence, for example, a 1a-2-3 individual will avoid being seen to be weak by fighting the source of the threat.

It is important to be clear that these are basic or "core" reactions. They will be associated with other responses, as part of a reaction "matrix", in any given situation. However, they are the *driving force* for each individual in any situation which is perceived to be a threat. Basically, we all have a strategy to avoid the situation that has caused us the most psychological pain in our early lives; and every time we are again confronted with one of these situations, we have a deeply ingrained physical, emotional and mental strategy for dealing with the problem.

Now let us look at the situation of any of these nine character structures within the context of financial markets. I don't think many would disagree if I isolated three specific characteristics of a financial market:

1 They are moving continuously;
2 There is an ever present risk of losing money;
3 They are subject to an infinite variety of influences.

The important point is that each individual is going to be particularly vulnerable to one of these three characteristics – every individual's defensive focus of attention (see Table 2) is likely to be energized by one of these three characteristics. Let me demonstrate this with reference to Table 4.

Table 4   Initial response to threat

Type	Avoids	Initial response to threat
1a-2-3	Being seen to be weak	Fight the situation
1p-2-3/		
1p-3-2	Getting involved in conflict	Withdrawal
1a-3-2	Any form of imperfection	Anger – usually suppressed
2-1a-3	Not being liked/recognised/loved	Dented pride
2-1p-3	Failing in chosen tasks	Deceive yourself and others that everything's OK
2-3-1p	Being just an ordinary person	Envy the success of others
3-2-1a	Having insufficient data about life	Mental retreat to gain time and space
3-1p-2	Making any wrong decisions	Fear
3-1a-2	Physical or psychological pain	Make plans to avoid situation

The first group of people consists of those who are primarily instinct-orientated. They will tend to have a very acute sense of self and will protect their personal space. They will seek either to control or avoid anything which might intrude into this space. In order to maintain their security, the world is mentally classified into two parts; the part which is unchanging and unthreatening; and that part which is active and therefore a potential threat.

Financial markets are moving all the time. They are full of unseen individuals, who will deal for reasons that cannot be discerned.

Instinct-orientated individuals will therefore be confronted with that which they fear the most – an uncontrollable or intrusive environment. They will react to losses with a desire to fight the market, or with a withdrawal of attention and emotions, or with suppressed anger.

None of these reactions are appropriate for successful trading. First, trying to fight the market when it goes against you, boils down to thinking that you are right and the markets are wrong. This may well be true in the long run; but as Lord Keynes said: In the long run we are all dead! Second, a withdrawal of attention in order to avoid anger, implies continuing to run bad positions, which could become very much worse. Eventually, the failure to take account of what has been going on, forces the individual to turn to others for help. Third, the process of suppressing anger means that important energy resources are going to be diverted away from coping with the market; stress is increased; and efficient trading is reduced. Ultimately, all that remains is an overwhelming sense of inadequacy and guilt.

The second group of people consists of those who are driven by their feelings. These individuals are motivated by the need to protect their self-image and will focus attention on gaining approval from others. Feelings of low self-esteem are generated when this approval is not forthcoming. Unfortunately, such feelings of low self-esteem often derive from the fact that – in Western culture anyway – we are trained from childhood not to make mistakes. People who have responded the most actively to this sort of training are basically afraid to make mistakes because it makes them feel unattractive, and the natural drive to find out about the world may even become suppressed.

Financial markets continuously present the danger, and the reality, of losing money. In fact, nobody can trade with a 100% success record. Feeling-centred individuals will therefore invariably be confronted with that which they desire least – namely, loss-making trades. The reaction is likely to be a sense of hurt pride, envy of others who are more successful, or a false pretence that it's OK really.

Again, none of these reactions are conducive to successful trading in financial markets. Attention is diverted away from coping with the reality of a loss-making trade towards coping with ego problems. First, hurt pride usually triggers hostility towards the market and may involve trying to take revenge on the market by adding to loss-making trades. Second, focusing attention on the success of others, which thereby highlights one's own inadequacies, can only lead to a withdrawal from markets and to missing opportunities to make amends. Third, ignoring the message of the loss, and pretending that the position will come right, forces the individual to turn to others for help.

The third group of people involves those who are characterized by thinking. Individuals in this general category are prone to experience fear very acutely and are therefore motivated by the desire to minimize fear. Such people will focus their attention on information and will be acutely aware of information that constitutes a threat. The greatest threat to security is that of making a loss; and individuals who seek to avoid losses are faced with the need to analyze an almost infinite quantity of information.

Financial markets therefore confront thought-orientated individuals with precisely the situation they most want to avoid – uncertainty. The result is to delay making decisions for as long as possible, to be frozen with fear and to ignore threatening information when a decision goes wrong, or to avoid the issue either by making plans about future trading or by doing other things.

Yet again, none of these reactions is appropriate for successful trading. First, any delay in taking a decision is likely to result in a missed opportunity or in higher-than-necessary losses. Eventually the trader may be driven to frenetic action in a vain attempt to recoup losses. Second, to be frozen by fear when a situation goes wrong means that the situation is likely to become much worse. Ultimately, relief from fear will only be obtained by an aggressive cutting out of loss-making positions. Third, to pretend that the problem does not exist is merely to delay the day of reckoning. In the meantime, the trader may be forced into a phase of quite obsessive perfectionism in order to avoid dealing with the problem.

To summarize, the critical problem is that *financial markets are continuously generating all the most potent threats for every single individual all the time.*

Consequently, the maximum number of people are feeling

threatened all the time. This in turn means that, despite promises of infinite wealth for the successful trader, the real experience is different. For the vast majority of people, the actual or potential emergence of losses is likely to generate negative emotions and inappropriate defensive strategies.

It does not take a genius to recognize that these defensive strategies are unlikely to rectify the situation. Put bluntly, as stress increases, the attitude towards dealing becomes less and less rational. Furthermore, personal psychological stability can become severely threatened. Incorrect decisions are therefore likely to mount and personal life satisfaction is likely to deteriorate. Inevitably, the trader will seek relief from the anxiety by identifying with other traders with similar views. In other words, a herding instinct is triggered. This may seem surprising, because it is not immediately obvious. But the herding together is primarily a psychological process, not a physical one. Nature has endowed us with a "Janus" type character. On the one hand, we present ourselves to the world as individuals; on the other hand, we have a powerful – and usually unrecognized – desire to belong to a group of some sort. In one sense, we are no different to any other element of Nature; every unit has an individual identity but every unit also participates in greater wholes.

Research has shown that the need to belong to a greater social grouping is not only very fundamental, but is intensified if there is a perceived threat of some sort. Financial markets create conditions that are potentially threatening for every trader.

In my book *Forecasting Financial Markets*, I have described how the threat of losses, and a feed-back relationship between price movements and dealing activity, causes individuals to coalesce into a higher-level, self-organizing, crowd. Rising prices stimulate the unpleasant feelings associated with the fear of being left out of the market. This encourages traders to do as others have done and buy the market. Alternatively, falling prices stimulate the unpleasant feelings associated with the fear of being left in the market. This encourages traders to join the crowd and sell the market. As a trend develops, the strength of the crowd mind intensifies. A crowd controls its subordinate parts and behaves, in total, just like any other organism in Nature. While it is in existence, a financial market crowd will therefore behave according to natural laws. In my opinion, the natural laws relating to financial market crowds dictate that:

1 The energy in the crowd will vibrate in a cyclical manner; that
2 These energy vibrations reflect a very distinct three-phase wave pattern (The "Price Pulse" – see "Forecasting Financial Markets"), which reproduces itself at all levels of the market's time-hierarchy; and that
3 Each phase of this wave pattern will tend to be mathematically related to other phases by some variation of the Golden Measure 1.618.

These laws create all the phenomena known to technical analysis – namely, price cycles, specific price patterns, and calculable price targets. In other words, it is precisely the phenomenon of the crowd that validates the use of technical analysis.

The question is: how can individuals overcome their avoidance compulsions and evade the magnetic pull of the crowd so that they can trade successfully in financial markets? Part of the solution of course is to adopt a decision-making process – a trading system – which generates buy and sell signals on an objective basis. In principle, the use of such a system gives the trader the potential to separate himself or herself from the herd.

However, the use of a trading system is not a sufficient condition for success. It is a necessary condition, but only provides the working tools. The difficulty is that any system which allows a trader literally to see the recent move in prices automatically exposes the trader to the essential catalyst of the "crowd" mentality – namely moving prices themselves.

A recent approach to this problem has therefore been to try and break the circular link between moving prices and negative emotions by psychological re-structuring or "re-engineering" (of the trader him/herself). Indeed a whole new "self-help" industry has emerged to deal with this problem. Available techniques range from training courses using neuro-linguistic programming (NLP), through individual hypnotherapy, to books, videos and tapes.

The great value of these techniques is not just that they focus attention on the problems of trading; they also enhance self-awareness. In this context, I would certainly recommend an excellent article on the subject by Van K. Tharp and Henry O. Pruden ("The Ten Tasks of Top Trading"), which was published in the 1994 *IFTA Journal*.

I would counsel, however, that most of the psychological programming techniques can, at best, only be "surface structure". That is, they can only deal with the suppression or circumvention of low-level fears. They cannot eliminate the "deep structure" avoidance compulsions which have been outlined in this article; and the great danger is that the compulsions will erupt when they are least expected. The important point is that it is essential to be aware of an avoidance compulsion as it emerges in order to disempower it to some extent.

If, therefore, a trader adopts a structured approach to the task of trading along the lines recommended by Tharp and Pruden and seeks to isolate his or her character bias as defined by this article, then the chances of success are very high.

Unfortunately though, avoidance compulsions are lifetime bandits and they will always lurk in the hills waiting to bushwhack us!

Tony Plummer is a director at Guiness Flight Hambros Global Fund Managers and is responsible for trading currencies and Sterling Bonds. He has been using TA since 1979. He published the book *Forecasting Financial Markets* in 1989 (published as *The Psychology of Technical Analysis* in the USA). This book is now on its third edition and has been translated into a number of languages. Tony is also a qualified NLP Practitioner.

Appendix 3

RECOMMENDED READING

Essential

Anonymous (1975), *A Course in Miracles,* Foundation for Inner Peace.

Brown, Constance (1995), *Aerodynamic Trading,* New Classics Library.

Douglas, Mark (1990), *The Disciplined Trader,* New York Institute of Finance.

Elder, Alexander (1993), *Trading for a Living,* Kogan Page.

Hill, Napoleon (1987), *Think and Grow Rich,* Fawcett Crest.

Lefevre, Edwin (1994), *Reminiscences of a Stock Operator,* John Wiley & Sons (it's all in here)

Niederhoffer, Victor (1997), *The Education of a Speculator,* John Wiley & Sons (yes, an excellent book, but reading his trading anecdotes will explain why the fund went bust!).

Plummer, Tony (1993), *Forecasting Financial Markets,* Kogan Page.

Robbins, Anthony (1992), *Awaken the Giant Within,* Simon & Schuster.

Steidlmayer, Peter (1990), *New Market Discoveries,* Kirbmarn.

Toghraie, Adrienne and Bernstein, Jake (1995), *The Winning Edge,* Target *TTT* Newsletters.

Van Tharp, Dr (1990), *Peak Performance Course.*

Williams, Bill (1995), *Trading Chaos,* John Wiley & Sons.

Others

Schwager, Jack (1989), *Market Wizards (I & II),* Harper & Row.

Toppel, Edward Allen (1992), *Zen in the Markets,* Warner Bros.

Ross, Joe (1994), *Trading by the Minute,* Trading Educators Ltd.

Sloman, James (1990), *Nothing,* IIT.

I also particularly recommended the *Market Profile Study Guide* (1991) published by and available from Chicago Board of Trade (CBOT) for $150 (inc. P&P). You can contact CBOT on US 312.341.7016, fax 312.347.3888.

Proscribed list

All books on Elliott and Gann.

TRADING AND PSYCHOLOGY QUESTIONNAIRE

by Tony Plummer, MSTA

This questionnaire is extensive in its scope. The more fully you answer the various questions the more useful will be the feedback we can give you. However this is not intended to be an interrogation and if you do not wish to answer any questions please just state by the side of that question '"NO ANSWER PROVIDED" or 'NAP" for short. Some answers require more than just a single word, in these cases feel free to use a separate sheet, but please reference each such anwer to the question to which it relates. The questions are deliberately not standarized, so you are free to answer (or not) as you see fit.

Also this questionnaire is designed to show you insights into your trading and as such it may pay you to spend some time in completing this. It should prove time well spent. Do not rush it. Please e-mail me (see page 240 for contact details) if you would like my feedback on your answers.

Trading

A Motivation

1 What do you want from markets?

2 How are you going to get it?

3 What will you then have? Describe your expected emotions.

4 What will you then want?

5 How are you going to get it?

6 What will you then have? Describe your expected emotions.

7 Repeat questions 4–6 in sequence until you reach a final answer.

8 What do you see as your primary reason for trading markets?

9 Do you have any secondary reasons?

10 Might the need for additional challenges have some part to play in the reason you trade markets?

11 Might boredom and the need to relieve it have some part to play in the reason you trade markets?

12 Might the need for excitement have some part to play in the reason you trade markets?

13 Might ego stimulation have some part to play in the reason you trade markets?

14 Might self-esteem have some part to play in the reason you trade markets?

15 Is it possible that some or other of these emotions trigger you into trades at some points?

16 What do you see as other reasons that you take trades you ought not to take?

17 Which trading vehicles do you prefer? Stocks/Options/Futures*

18. Do you ever find yourself being unable to take trades?

19 What do you feel may be the reasons for this?

20 In monetary terms what are your goals in the market?

21 Do you see these as realistic?

22 Would you be able to achieve these goals whilst staying "cool, calm and collected"?

23 In view of your answers to questions 21 and 22, do you want to modify your reply to question 20?

Ring the appropriate option.

B Experience

1 Most traders wipe out before they learn the all important lesson to limit losses. Have you been through this experience? *yes/no

2 Please give details (write on a separate sheet if need be).

3 Describe the emotions associated with this event.

4 What do you think you learnt?

5 Do you feel that you have dealt with this experience fully?

6 Describe the fears that you now encounter trading markets?

7 List the trading actions you will not take. For example, not holding overnight, not trading futures or writing options etc.

8 Do you see these as limitations?

9 What sort of stops do you like to use?

10 Do you use specific methodologies?

11 Do you have solely one such or more than one? Give number.

12 Does this methodology give you precise entry/exit signals?

13 If not why not?

14 Do you think the reasons given under "13" above are a positive or a negative to your trading success?

15 As a result of your answer to "14" above do you intend to take any action?

16 Why not?

17 Do you think that if your methodology was more precise that you would learn more about why you sometimes take inappropriate trading signals?

18 Do you think inappropriate means anything to do with resultant profits or losses?

19 If so, why?

20 Do you use profit targets?

21 If so, why?

22 Do you have experience trading both futures and options?

23 Would you prefer a 10% chance of making £10 000 or a 90% chance of making £1000. Would it make any difference if the 90% chance was for £1100 not just £1000?

24 How do you feel after a string of five losses?

25 When you lose is it usually the fault of someone else? Please explain.

26 Do you frequently take your broker's advice on the markets?

27 If so what are the results?

28 Do you examine your brokerage statements carefully?

Ring the appropriate option.

C Results

1 Do you make losses overall?

2 If so are you trading more than a single contract?

3 Do you see any logic in continuing to do so?

4 Do your losses arise from lots of small losses or a few big losses?

NB: It is sometimes said that novice traders make a few big losses (because they fail to take small losses quickly), more experienced traders make many small losses (because they put stops too tight). An adjunct to this is that very experienced derivative fund managers often lose in absolute terms because their clients take money away when they lose, thus they make money on smaller sums than when they lose money.

5 Do you think your problems stem from inexperience or from fear?

6 Or do you attribute this to other factors?

7 Do you take full responsibility for your trading actions and results?

8 If not, who is responsible?

9 Do your profits come from many small profits, or a few big profits? If you are not yet profitable which do you feel will apply to you?

10 Do you buy on good news?

11 If so, why?

12 Is it rare that the markets cause you any major problems?

13 Do you only ever lose what you plan in the markets?

14 When you lose more, are there good reasons? Please list.

15 If a great opportunity arises will you risk most of your money on it?

16 Explain why most traders are fugitives from the law of averages.

17 Do you love the thrill of trading, whether you win or lose?

18 Is trading your hobby?

19 If you lose do you want to get back at the market?

20 Do you usually act impulsively?

21 Do you hold your investments through thick and thin, do you have no problem holding in a bear market?

22 Do you talk about your trading results to anyone?

23 Do you keep a clear written record of all your trades and results?

24 Do you keep a journal listing all the reasons why you open and close trades?

25 If not, why not?

26 Are you a net loser over the last five years (or less if you have been trading for less than five years)?

D Perception

1 Should a good system produce profits each month?

2 If the dartboard method works would you use it?

3 Do you regularly follow the advice of others?

4 Are you often confused?

5 Do you feel you have to be an insider to win?

6 Do you feel worthless unless you win?

7 Will you do a lot not to upset your broker?

8 Do you believe in random trading?

9 An orang-utan at London zoo is calling the market with 86% accuracy. Do you follow the ape?

10 If you had to liken the market to an animal, real, imaginary or otherwise, what animal would it be?

11 What is your view of market systems?

12 Do you believe that once you find "your" system you will be successful?

13 Or do you believe that once you become a good trader that everything else will follow?

14 Have you mapped out the trading objectives you need to achieve? I do not mean financial targets, I mean the lessons you need to learn. As an example it may run, learn to cut losses, develop a methodology, learn to follow it, learn to run profits, become expert in this approach.

15 List those things you feel have meaning in the market.

16 How do you use these to make money?

E Current situation

1 Could you live off your investments at this time?

2 How much time do you have for the market?

3 Do you ever miss trades because you are not paying sufficient attention?

4 How do you feel about that?

5 Do you get emotionally involved with the market?

6 If so, to what extent?

7 Is this useful?

8 What action do you propose to avoid this problem?

9 Are you often compelled to trade?

10 Do you often feel no need to trade?

11 How many contracts are you trading?

12 When you lose on a trade what percentage of your capital is lost?

13 Explain why you think this is the right level of risk for you?

14 Explain the statistical implications of this level of risk?

15 How many winning trades do you make on average, as a percentage of your trades in total.

16 Explain the statistical implications of this percentage allied to your level of risk.

17 Do you overspend?

18 What percentage of your capital is involved in trading?

Personal

1 Do you and your partner ever argue?

2 Do you enjoy meeting new people?

3 Are you a winner?

4 Are most of your friends winners also?

5 Do you ever lie?

6 Do you regularly list your goals, trading and otherwise?

7 Do you feel it is unlikely that you will attain any of your goals?

8 Do you have many close friends?

9 Is there anything that you are afraid to talk about?

10 Do you like everyone you know?

11 Do you love everyone you know?

12 When you do something do you dislike others to benefit?

13 Do you eat too much?

14 Do you smoke too much?

15 Do you drink alcohol to excess?

16 Do you take drugs to excess?

17 Do you engage in other self destructive behavior?

18 Do you not know why?

19 If you answered yes to any of questions 13 to 18 it would be useful if you gave more details. But do not feel obliged to do so.

20 Do you get on well with your work colleagues?

21 Do your work colleagues like you?

22 Do you regularly take holidays?

23 Have you ever felt better than you do now?

24 Do you more often see (a) other people's uses or (b) other people's viewpoints?

25 Do you feel uncomfortable going against the majority view?

26 If everyone in a room had removed their shoes would you do the same?

27 Are you afraid to face the reality of yourself?

28 Are you in touch with your own feelings?

29 Are you under pressure to succeed, either from yourself or others?

30 Are you relaxed when you trade?

31 Are you jealous of anyone?

32 In a confused situation would you turn to another for advice?

33 Why?

34 Is wealth important to you?

35 How would you define being wealthy?

36 How much time do you spend on newspapers?

37 What do they do for you?

38 Do you equate money to love?

39 If so, why?

40 Are you fit?

41 What exercise do you do?

42 Do you feel that it is important to be physically fit to trade markets?

43 If so why?

44 What does money mean to you?

Appendix 5

IS ELLIOTT ADDICTIVE?

This is a story about my own experiences with the Elliott Wave Theory. I think it illustrates a number of important points about the way in which many people (including me) use different techniques and the dangers that can befall them. My story may not be typical in some ways, but in others I am sure it is.

I cannot recall precisely how I got hold of it, but I started to take Bob Beckman's *Investors Bulletin*. In 1985/86, I think, I got hold of his book *Super Timing* which deals with the Elliott Wave Theory. Now this is a good book and the rest of this appendix is not to suggest otherwise.

I started to study this technique and it had immediate appeal. This is probably a personal thing but the patterns seemed interesting and had the obvious attraction of apparently identifying tops and bottoms of importance. Perhaps I ought to say that at this point I was very much a novice. I was also reading *Investor's Bulletin* and was also convinced that the market was going to fall back – I was definitely a bear at that time – and I had no idea about such things (views) being dangerous – that thought never even occurred to me.

So I tried to use Elliott and it worked fairly well, such that I continued to identify patterns. I bought (I said I was a novice) a few puts and most expired valueless but then one did well. I got out early (of course) but still covered my previous losses – Yes! I was hooked. Then I had a conversation with a friend who told me how you could write options. Later, whilst skiing in Avoriaz, I considered this technique and I couldn't see how it could fail. You sell some calls and if it goes up you sell some puts, if it goes down again you sell more calls. The wonders of margin and the perils of doubling position size were unknown to me at that time. This continued though 1986 and into 1987. I won some, I lost some. My business at that time was going well and my position size kept growing – it frightens me now to think back and realise the extent to which I was overtrading – but back then I was in blissful ignorance. Then came the 1987 Crash. Was this my undoing? Perhaps, but not in the way you might think. Remember I was a bear, and I was a bear hooked on Elliott.

I have previously shown a chart of the 1987 Crash but it is the perfect illustration to this appendix and so Figure V.1 shows the 1987 Crash once again. Look at the perfection of that Elliott pattern, the five wave decline off the August peak. The obvious corrective move into the October peak and then the resolution of this pattern – perfect! Not only that, but the move was heralded by hurricanes throughout the South of England.

Of course my trading through this period was not perfect. I had 60 long puts the week before the Crash, plus a number of short calls. I managed to close 40 of the puts the week before the Crash (brilliant eh?) and the remainder on the morning of the Crash thus missing out on the best part

Fig V.I   Why Elliott is addictive

of the move. This despite that fact that I was predicting a move in excess of 300 points – following that perfect pattern. But I was also using a five hour RSI and when it got oversold out I got – aren't these indicators wonderful!

The week before the Crash I had a relatively long conversation with a "Gann" expert and we compared notes. We were both expecting FTSE to fall back but when I mentioned 300 points, he said something like "Oh No, more like 100!" I often wonder how he felt when he got the 300 points in one day, and another 300 the day after.

However, consider the impact of this forecast on a novice bear – and that is what this appendix is all about. The market reinforced my attraction to Elliott in the most powerful way possible and this early on in the sequence when I was the most impressionable. The market showed me that it is possible to forecast the future (it isn't), it showed me how accurate Elliott is (it has never given a call as good as that one since), and it has shown how good a view can be (a view is often fatal).

Now let's take a step back and consider other alternatives which can befall us as we start down the road towards trading success – not that many of us actually reach that goal – "many are called but few are chosen! "(Matthew 20:16) There are a number of possible outcomes. However these can be classified into three main groupings. The first grouping is where the initial analysis technique (in my case Elliott) is found to be "defective." In this case the trader will probably switch to another technique. The second grouping is what we might term as "modestly successful." Here the trader will still lose money because of shortcomings but he may still get hooked on this technique. The third grouping we might term as "very successful" and I think this is what happened to me. This can be the worst of all because then the technique can become truly addictive.

In all cases traders need to become familiar with a large number of techniques if only so that they can dismiss them. But they also need to become expert in the techniques which give them what they want. What they don't need is to become hooked on something and in this respect failure in the early stages is probably more useful than anything else. Especially when you consider that early success, before an understanding of Money Management is obtained, can easily lead to trading greatly increased sums with inevitable doomsday consequences.

However another point in this sequence has recently been graphically illustrated to me. This concerns "Market Profile."

I was introduced to "Market Profile" by a stockbroker about six years or so ago. At the time I read the book he recommended and it made absolutely no impact on me. It seemed to me to be just a different way of displaying the same information. What I completely missed was the handle on "Value" which this technique provides and how useful minus development can be. Now this is a fairly important point. I do not consider myself much better than average in assimilating information but trading is my profession and if I read about a technique I would expect to glean at least the essential features – but in this case I did not. This is a little worrying. Does it mean that every book I read I approach with my subjective views firmly in place and am thus unable to see the value which might lie therein? This is clearly so, and if I do this it is likely that we all do the same in greater or lesser degree. If this is true, and I think it is undoubtedly so, then we will only take in what we are ready for – although another way of putting this is what we want to take in. This means that we are even more responsible for our actions than we might have thought because if we control our input, as we do, we also control the way we are and thus how we react to all stimuli which ultimately means our actions and what happens to us.

This is particularly true of trading. So it might be that you have already discovered the technique which would suit you best but, for a variety of reasons, you may have dismissed it. I have certainly found "Market Profile" extremely useful now that I can see it operating in real time. Of course when you can watch a "master" using a technique to make money in the markets it does tend to make a lot more sense than just reading a book about the subject.

So the position is more complicated than merely getting to know a technique, you must also beware of failing to get to know a technique. To an extent getting in tune with "your" techniques, i.e. the ones which will ultimately bring you to success, is a matter of asking the right questions. When we start out trading we don't know enough to frame these questions. If asked what we consider to be the most important aspects leading to trading success we might ramble on about key indicators, or following a successful trader, or some pet theory. But we probably wouldn't mention psychology, or low risk trading ideas, or even stops. To a large extent the early years are spent learning the basics as happens in any apprenticeship. It is purely arrogance and ignorance which leads successful and intelligent people to feel that they will be able to trade markets with success right from the off – and I am not being "holier than thou" here because I was just the same. But this is clearly foolish and the markets extract their pound of flesh in return.

So it is important to review your progress to date. Review the knowledge you have acquired to ensure, as far as possible, that you have got the most out of what you know and that you have not become hooked on anything. Review in particular what you want out of your techniques and whether you are getting it. Review whether the trades you take are "low risk opportunities" and if not consider how to change your techniques so that they become such – because that is essential!

THE FORTUNE STRATEGY

As a trader my concern is to place profitable trades. As a writer I have two goals: one is to write a book that is going to be useful, not to mention interesting, the other, and perhaps the primary goal of any writer, is to be read. It is fairly obvious when you think about it. Writing a book is a lot of work. I don't mind hard work but I do like to have achieved something at the end of it – it is very gratifying to receive letters and emails telling me I have done just that!

So when it came to this new edition it was very much in my mind that the book had worked well the first time round (indeed, over 10,000 people read the book). Plus, for my part, there is nothing I have experienced in markets since 1998 which have led me to want to revise any of my previous conclusions.

That is not to say that I have not kept writing. Indeed I am now on my fifth book – I have always had an addictive personality, the key is to channel the addictions into useful activities!

So in this new edition I decided to introduce my second book – *The Fortune Strategy* – and say a few words about markets today.

First *The Fortune Strategy* - this new book has a very different premise and that premise is to have a plan to make markets work for you. In my consultancy work I meet and work with many traders and they often lack any clear idea of where they are going. Yet having a clear plan is one of the essentials when it comes to the markets. *The Fortune Strategy* provides just such a plan, but it goes further. It also gives clear guidance as to how to develop your own system. Again, in my consultancy work, this is one of the key obstacles facing traders, they have no idea how to develop their system, the system which they need to express their trading personality.

So here are two extracts from the book. I have chosen these chapters as they extend some of the ideas discussed in *The Way to Trade*:

FIRST EXTRACT - MILESTONES

Learning to trade is a complex achievement. Perhaps surprisingly there are many similarities between this and learning to excel in other areas such as show jumping and mountain climbing. I realise that this may seem a little far-fetched and I fully appreciate the many differences. Trading involves sitting in a room watching a screen. Actually it doesn't but that is the physical manifestation. The other two involve a very physical activity in the open air involving personal danger and risk, but strip away the physical aspects and look at the effects on the brain. In all cases we are faced with learning skills which involve much risk and which will thus stir emotion and instinct.

Becoming a good trader, a good rider or a good climber all involve dealing with these aspects first and foremost. We do not take on knowledge to make progress, we lose certain fears. To a large extent the first step is unlearning responses which are not helpful. We need to strip ourselves to the bone and then re-build ourselves in a more useful format.

I became aware of this recently when I was talking to a trainer of Olympic show jumpers. I was surprised how much similarity there is between the two functions. In another sense all these activities, and other similar challenges, mean we have to transcend ourselves. We are taking on something bigger than we are, be it a horse, a mountain, or a market. The basic formula I often mention holds true. We start off emotionally, we then learn to behave mechanically (eliminating the emotional and instinctive input) and then we become expert. This is equally true of horse riding, trading and even applies to spiritual paths.

As a trader all this is only of passing interest because I have now reached my goal and I make money consistently, but as a trading coach it is absolutely vital, as it should be to anyone who is still struggling to make money.

Whilst talking to the show jumping trainer two other points arose. First that some of us develop "advanced conceptual skills". I have yet to absorb this fully but apparently unless we study physics or mathematics before the age of 15 we do not develop these skills. I was talking about my trading strategy of writing options and hedging with futures and apparently this would not make sense to anyone without these advanced conceptual skills. This had never occurred to me before and why should it? In common with most other human beings I tend to think other people are generally like myself. It never occurred to me that I might have skills others do not, and cannot possess, but then I am useless at languages, others find them easy. The truth is we are, in fact, all different; neither better nor worse, simply different.

However we think we are the same and if you listen carefully, you will hear people describe themselves, because what they think you are, they are very likely themselves. For example, if anyone doubts anything I say my automatic assumption is that that person cannot be trusted. They are showing me that they are untrustworthy, thus they think others are the same.

What is the implication of the differences between people? Simply what I have always said; each trader must develop his own trading personality, and it is no coincidence that this is the subtitle to my book *The Way To Trade*. We all have different strengths and weaknesses and our trading personality must be such as to maximise the effect of our strengths and minimise the effects of our weaknesses.

The second point arose because the trainer could not understand how some riders seemed to have "natural" ability. This was obviously of great concern to him as it might provide a wealth of information as to how to improve his techniques. His conclusion is that this may be a genetic effect, that great riders can pass this through to their offspring through their genes. I have a different theory. I think we learn much better when we are young. We have not developed all the mental garbage that gets in the way of us and our achievement. At that point children see things far more clearly, thus when they observe their parent riding exceptionally well, they pick up on the key points, and go and do the same. Not immediately, but the basic structure is in place, just waiting to be developed. Those who have not been in the position to carefully view such peak skills in action regularly simply do not have the same hidden talents, and how could they? So I would say it is not genetics but simply observation at an early age. This has little relevance to trading as few traders start that young and I know few traders whose parents were great traders. Also how many children are going to be enthralled whilst their parent sits in front of a screen and occasionally picks up the phone? The skills of a trader are not very visual, but this concept might be useful in underlining the need for regular contact with someone who is successful. That is how the best learn in all other professions. Trading is no different.

I think this is an excellent introduction to my milestones, the key lessons I learnt along the way, which have brought me to where I am today. If I can convey to you the key decisions I took and how they affected my trading career, maybe I can help you along your way. The truth is that there are not that many of them. The key lessons are few.

Trading initiation

The first milestone must be the one that introduced me to the market. I think this can be summarised as curiosity, at least at first. At the time I was a tax consultant but I was not finding the work very inspiring. Part of the work involved investment and I used to read *Bob Beckman's Investors' Bulletin* (now sadly defunct or at least no longer involving Mr. Beckman). This led me to buy his book *Supertiming* on the Elliott Wave Theory. I started to apply this to the market and built up an interest in the way FTSE moved. However this was not what got me hooked. That came from a different quarter. A friend (fiend?) of mine explained that you could write options as well as buying them. I didn't see how I could lose. I overlooked the problems of margin and the danger of doubling position size. Two small obstacles which turned a sure thing into an eventual nightmare. I cannot say whether my main reason for trading was money or whether it was the challenge, and the excitement. I suspect the challenge and the excitement were more pressing reasons with the rewards a good underlying basis for going ahead. Most of the big things we do in life have a number of reasons behind them.

The realisation that you have to cut losses

Having started to trade what was my first milestone along the way? I can only think of one that stands out and that is to limit losses. Maybe it took me longer to realise this because I was writing options right from the start and I had never even heard of futures. It seems incredible now but in the 1980s futures were far less popular, indeed many of the contracts we have today did not even exist then. With options I was very quick to hedge positions by selling more options. This became very expensive and I only fully learnt the right lessons when I switched to futures trading. For me this was an essential step which, in turn, led to my adopting mechanised approaches.

The realisation that this is not easy, that a lot of hard work is required

As with the first realisation this one did not come in all at once but took time to make itself obvious...

SECOND EXTRACT - A QUESTION OF BALANCE - THE KEY FACTORS DETERMINING OVERALL SUCCESS IN THE MARKETS

Everyone who is involved with markets wants to come out a winner; this chapter outlines the four essential areas that separate the winners from the losers. These points are as applicable to investors as they are to traders.

There is nothing revolutionary herein; most of this is well known to investors and traders. Indeed it is too well known, because the best place to hide a secret is where everyone can see it, that way they do not realise its worth. These four factors are more than simple rules for success; they also mark the path through success. Without more ado here are the four:

1. Cut your losses.
2. Run your profits.
3. Trade selectively.
4. Maintain good balance.

There are four stages of development which we all go through in any endeavour to reach success, these are:

1. Novice
2. Intermediate
3. Expert
4. Master

In my book *The Way to Trade*, I dealt with the first three exhaustively and showed how to develop the right mind set for success by using the model I developed which I call **The Trading Pyramid**. However I did not deal with the fourth factor, balance. Balance is more than just an additional rule it must also become one of the levels of the pyramid itself.

Novice traders and investors come to the market without much idea of what they are getting involved in, and with the view that they will have an easy ride, producing lots of lovely profits. Invariably they will get a rude awakening, what we might call a reality shock. This is when they learn to cut losses and it is this lesson which marks the move to intermediate status ...

The Fortune Strategy is now available from Global Investor http://books.global-investor.com/books/23374.htm If you found *The Way to Trade* interesting, useful and worthwhile then I am sure you will also enjoy *The Fortune Strategy*. Receive it for £49.95 instead of the usual price of £89.95 – that is a discount of 44%, simply mention that you have previously purchased The Way to Trade to receive the discount.

MARKETS TODAY

In The Way to Trade I state one truth. That markets move from extreme to extreme across all time frames. I also added, at the end of the Epilogue to the original book, "but I do know that an extreme high will be seen at some point..."

The main Global equity markets all peaked between September 1999 and March 2000 – not so long after I made that statement. Since then we have seen some major falls with the NASDAQ 100 leading the pack with a 83.5% decline off the top.

One interesting point about these peaks was that the UK FTSE 100 index peaked on the last trading session of 1999, just as the Nikkei Dow peaked on the last trading session 10 years earlier. This is no coincidence and is in fact a perfect example of an "emotional" high – see page 153. Markets are a manifestation of popular psychology and the index is a good measure of the "feel good" factor in society at any one time. When is that feel good factor at a peak? Very often on New Year's Eve when we celebrate the year gone and look forward to the coming year – and in 1999 it was not just the New Year we were looking forward to but the New Millennium!

I do not think proof is needed that markets are a measure of popular psychology; but if proof were needed here it is. Of course markets do not always peak on such occasions, the forces affecting stock prices are complex and many, but if I had to choose a day for a peak, that would be it.

Once markets peaked they fell back to extreme lows and then rallied. The extreme lows came in between October 2002 and March 2003. Some of these rallies are now threatening to take markets back to new all time highs. Indeed some markets are bound to see such highs although probably not the NASDAQ which by January 2006 had only managed to retrace 24% of the previous fall.

Such a weak retracement over a three-year period suggests all we are seeing here is a bear market rally and that we have more downside to come. Clearly the lows seen between October 2002 and March 2003 were an extreme in a major time frame but I do not think they were an extreme in the same time frame as the all time peaks a few years before.

THE P/E RATIO ON THE S&P

A s evidence of this I would point to this long-term chart of the S&P
and its P/E ratio.

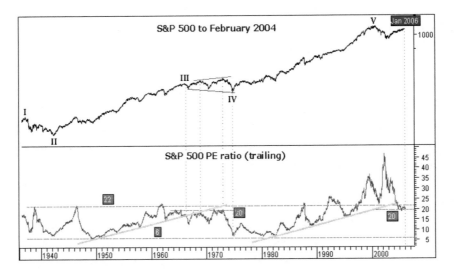

At the bottom of a big bear market P/E ratios are generally below 10.
This chart shows the P/E ratio on the S&P 500 since 1936. You will
notice how it stayed within a "normative" range right through from
around 1936 until the early 1990's. Then it went into hyper drive and
this is one of the reasons why I, and others, were so sceptical about that
huge bull run in the late 1990's – it was built on thin air! Hot thin air.
(thanks to Tim Wood of www.cycleman.com for this chart and to Bill
Adlard of http://www.chart-guide.com for the updating and
annotations)

All the collapse that we saw between 2000 and 2003 has done is bring
the P/E back to the top of the normative range. The long-term mean for
this P/E ratio is around 15 and we haven't even got down to that level
yet. Let along made it below 10 – traditionally where bear markets
terminate.

So all that collapse did was wipe away the froth, we still have to go
further down to complete a full bear market. We have seen Phase I and
Phase II, when the bad news hits the fan, may soon begin and this is

when earnings will also decline giving us a double whammy. Declining earnings will take price down but sentiment will take them down much further. Finally Phase III will take the market into deeply oversold territory – at this point expect there to be a general distrust of equity investment as we saw in the 1940s and 1950s. There is also likely to be comment that the capitalist system has failed. But there is probably no need for concern, it has happened before and will happen again – the key thing is to be prepared.

I consider the P/E ratio to be one of the best guides to the real state of the market. By looking at where the market is in comparison to its **long-term** mean you know a lot about where you are and where you are going. Remember markets always go back to the **long-term** mean and beyond!

If we link this tool to a simple trend following system we will be right more often than wrong. We will be looking at the very big moves because the P/E ratio is no good for short-term timing purposes but as an indication of what is to come it is unparalleled.

Bear Markets go through three phases

I mentioned these three phases above. Here is a summary:

1. Phase one when the excess is wiped away – this is what I believe we have already seen.
2. Phase two when the bad news hits the market and takes it down and sentiment falls with it.
3. Phase three when the true panic hits and markets become truly under-valued. Fear is rampant and you will read that this is the end of the financial system as we know it – the UK saw such a move in the early 1970s.

If we do see a move from extreme "over-value" down to extreme "under-value" then clearly these three phases will have to occur although they may not be separate moves, but might link up in some way. However the first phase down, which we have already seen, did not cause much economic damage and this is one of the reasons why I expect there is more downside to come – the structural problems are still there!

I include property markets in this. Property markets are like all other markets; they are simply slower moving and also have more obvious asset backing.

There is one golden rule which applies to all markets and this is that once people start to buy purely because they see appreciation in the future, then that is a time to start to be concerned. When I say "purely" I mean that value is long gone, price is already too high. It happened in the dot.com bubble, the fundamentalists, who some call the funnymentalists, could find no value although some pretended they could and got prosecuted for it! The only rationale for buying shares that were grossly overvalued was that they would go up. And they did! But then they collapsed. I believe this is true of much UK and US property at this time.

STRUCTURAL PROBLEMS

These are the main financial problems we face:

1. Equity markets are extended and vulnerable
2. Property markets are extended and vulnerable
3. The twin US deficits are putting the $ under pressure
4. Personal debt is threatening continuing consumer spending which is keeping the economies of the US and the World going
5. The US is hugely in debt to the rest of the world and if any country decides it wants out that will start a slide in the $.

The dangerous part is that if any one of these five problems starts to unravel it could act as a catalyst for all five. For example vast sums have been take out of mortgage financing by consumers and this has allowed the US and UK economies to grow. There are signs that property appreciation is slowing and this is likely to reduce the scope for further borrowing. This might reduce consumer spending and start a mild recession. Property and stock markets then start to fall and this might unnerve those investing in US dollars, which might also take down US Bond markets. The $ starts to slide and suddenly it is all happening at once.

This is not a pleasant scenario and I think Alan Greenspan chose his departure date from the Fed fairly well!

CONCLUSION

Ultimately a trader looks for opportunities and he chooses how to define those opportunities. This definition includes his preferred time frame. My comments above refer to the biggest time frame and this may be of no great interest to many readers, indeed most readers. I have to say my own trading time frame is certainly shorter term – as you will gather from reading this book.

But a decline of the magnitude expected would affect us all. It is curious that this book first went to press shortly before the major peaks were seen in 1999 and 2000. Might history repeat itself and might this revised edition also predate a major peak by a few months?

John Piper

April 2006

FREE NEWS SHEET!

John Piper is now issuing a FREE news sheet. This will focus on the major trades offered by the key equity markets and every issue will include a trading tip. There will be two or three issues every month, except when John is spending some of his trading profits on holiday.

TO subscribe please send a blank email to jptt@aweber.com

Please note this is **NOT** The Technical Trader which is only available by subscription.

INDEX

10-step approach 199–205
  expertise 204
  fear 203
  methodologies 201–2
  practice 203
  running profits 204
  survival 200–1
  theory 202
  where am I now? 199
  where do I want to go? 200
55 steps 15–18
Aborted patterns 175–6, 191
Acceptance 107, 131, 176
Algorithms 35–6
Analysis 8, 80
  options 157–8
  type 85
Arbitrage 84
Asia 231

Bell curve 37, 79, 127, 128
Box 172–3
  models 21–2
  Plummer, Tony 22–4, 59, 79, 241–54
  structure 22–5
  and systems 78–80
  and trading rules 77–81
  triune 21, 22–5, 79, 242–3
  Williams, Bill 21, 22–5

Chaos 26, 59
Character
  avoidance compulsion 247–9
  and markets 246–52
  nine categories 243–7
  structures 244–7
  traits 243–7
  vulnerable spots 246–7
Chart tutorial 209–18
Clinton scandal 231
Coaches see Trading coaches
Commitment 4–5, 35–9
Consultancy service 204, 240
Contact details 240
Corrective action 177–8
Crowds in financial markets 252–3

Data display 71–2
Derivatives 84
Directional approach 84, 119–20
  options 155
Discipline 5–6, 41–5, 184
  and analysis 47
  loop 21
  and Money Management system 43
  and Risk Control 43
Disclaimer 185–6
Douglas, Mark 21, 111

Economic black holes 233–5
Elliott Wave Theory 36, 85, 136, 183–4, 195, 212–3, 215–6
  addiction to 269–73
  Elliott Fives 174–5, 190–1
Emotion 3–4, 12–13, 241–2
Entry
  methodology 87
  strategy 70
Exit 48
  methodology 87–8
  strategy 70, 131

Failed breakthroughs 169–71, 190
Failed re-tests 172, 190, 211
Fear 203
  orientation 11–12, 13–14
Financial pressure 6
Futures 68–9, 140–1, 191–3
  10-step approach 199–205
  and FTSE 140–1
  strategies 165–79
  trading signals 167–8
  and value 165, 176

Gann 85, 136, 195, 240
  Gann Swing Charts 158
Gap opens 166–9
  and Minus Development 168
Germany 234
Goat 169–71
Goose 166–9
Greed orientation 11, 12–13
Greenspan 231

Hedging 84, 185
  moving hedges 160–1
  options 155, 158–62, 185
  Rule of 25 159–62
Horse 176–7

Illusion 174–5, 195–6

Indicators 195–6
Initial balance 132
Initiative action 132
IOP 158
Iraq war 235
Irish peace process 234

Japan 234

Key levels 173–4
Kuala Lumpar 231

Long 119
Longer time frame participants 173–4
Losses 62–4
   cutting 13, 60
Low risk opportunities 122–3, 131, 209–18
LTCM 235–6

MACD 158
MACD 85, 195
Maclean, Paul 242
Market analysis *see* Analysis
Market Eye 50
Market Profile 36, 37–8, 71, 78, 108, 122, 127–9, 133–5, 176
   balance 127
   imbalance 127
   and longer time frame participants 173–4
   options analysis 158
   trading tips 136
   value 130–1, 134–5, 165, 176
Market techniques 195–6
Markets 231–6
   and character 246–52
   crowds in 242–3
   and motivation 3–4
   effect of news 55–7
   emotion in 13
   essentials 29–30
   human psychology 36, 241–54
   nature of 35–6
   observation of 69
   reasons for trading 3–4
   requirements for success in 88–90
   reviewing 212
   shocks 55–6
   signals 156
Methodology 83–93
   10-step approach 201–2
Minus Development 36, 37–8, 72, 79, 108, 122, 128, 130, 131, 151, 152, 168
Money Management 6–7, 47–51, 70, 85–7, 215
   and analysis 47
   and discipline 43

position size	49–50
services	240
Motivation	3–4, 13
Moving Averages	158
Neuro-linguistic-programming	98, 253
News	122, 196
effect on markets	55–7
Normal distribution *see* Bell curve	
Operation	95–9
problems with	97–9
set-up	96–7
Options	67
10-step approach	199–205
analysis	157–8
buying	68, 143–8
FTSE	146
hedging	155, 158–62, 185
in-the-money	142
out-of-the-money	142
pricing by market	141–3, 157
strategies	145–8, 155–63
trading campaign	221–9
writing	68, 121, 122, 143–8, 155, 157–8
Overnighter	181, 191
Paper trading	49–50
Patterns aborting	122
PDS	181, 191
Piano	173–4
Platypus	175–6
Plummer, Tony	21, 59, 79
model of brain structure	22–4
Troubled Trader	241–54
Position	
balanced	121
monitoring	50–1
size	49–50, 70, 120
Preconceived ideas	183
Pressure	6
Profits	
letting run	14, 64–5, 204
or losses	9, 101–3
Pruden, Henry O	253
Psychologists	97, 98
Psychology	36, 241–54
and markets	36
psychological areas	243–51
psychological pressure	6
psychological restructuring	253
questionnaire	257–67
and trading coaches	113–14

Questionnaire	257–67
Ranges	
range extension	132
trading	69
Real time price services	50
Rejection	107–10
Responsive action	132
Risk	
and option buying	143, 146
orientation	12, 14–15, 55
warning	185–6
Risk Control	6–7, 53–7, 87
and discipline	43
risks inherent in the market	55
risks inherent in the vehicle	54–5
unexpected forms of risk	55–7
Robbins, Anthony	192
Ross, Joe	8, 183
RSI divergence	195
Rule of	25 159–62
Russia	231, 234, 235
Schwager, Jack	241
Serbia	235
Set-up	96–7
Short	119
Signal	50
Snake	172
Spikes	72, 151–3
and acceptance	107, 131
chart tutorial	209–12
and stops	151
type	152–3
Spread trading	84
Square congestion	172–3
Steidlmayer, Peter	37, 71, 78, 79, 127
Stochastics	195
Stocks	139–40
Stops	13, 70, 131, 182, 185
and acceptance	107, 131
approaches	106–7
avoiding	105–6
hedging	185
and Minus Development	79
mental	106
necessity of	105–6
policies	70
and random-entry systems	79
and rejection	107–10
and spikes	151
and trend following	176
types	106

using	61–2
Straddles	84, 120, 155–6
Strategies	120-2
and character	247–52
and discipline	120
entry	70, 87
exit	70, 87
futures	165–79
options	145–8, 155–63
Sub-conscious	242
Systems	13, 181–7, 197, 240
Aborted patterns	191
and character	253
design	69–74
Elliott Five	190–1
essential elements	189–90
failed break	169–71, 190
failed re-test	172, 190, 211
and human brain	78
long-term	72–3
Overnighter	181, 191
Parameters	6, 8, 43–4, 67–75, 77–81
PDS	181, 191
random-entry	78–9
requirements 70–1	
short-term	72–3
Trend-Hunter	181, 191
TTT weekly system	74
V	190
when to use	189–93
XXX	190
Technical analysis software	240
Tenfore	50
Tharp, Van	111, 253
home study course	114–15
Three simple rules *see* Trading secrets	
Three stages	7
fear orientated	11–12, 13–14
greed orientated	11, 12–13
risk orientated	12, 14–15, 55
Time frames	84
and trends	69–70
Time Price Opportunities	71–2, 128–9, 130, 131, 134–5
Toghraie, Adrienne	111, 113–4
Trade selectivity	14–15, 60–1, 65
Trader	
evolution of	11–19
fear orientated	11–12, 13–14
greed orientated	11, 12–13
interview with institutional	88–93, 133–5
problems with operation	97–9
risk orientated	12, 14–15, 55

Trading chaos | 26, 59
Trading coaches | 97, 111–15
  benefits | 111–13
  Douglas, Mark | 111
  home study courses | 114–15
  Tharp, Van 111, | 253
  Toghraie, Adrienne | 111
Trading Pyramid | 101–3
  commitment | 4–5, 35–9
  discipline | 5–6, 41–5, 184
  introduction | 3–9
  methodology | 83–93
  Money Management | 6–7, 47–51
  operation | 95–9
  overview of levels | 4–9
  personalizing | 213–14
  profits or losses | 9
  Risk Control | 6–7, 53–7
  System Parameters | 6, 8, 43–4, 67–75, 77–81
  three simple rules | 59–66
  you | 4, 29–32
Trading secrets | 7, 31, 69–66
  cutting your losses | 13, 60, 62–4
  and human brain | 77–81
  letting profits run | 14, 60, 64–5, 204
  trade selectivity | 14–15, 60–1, 65
  trading with the trend | 61, 65
  using | 61–5
Trading
  and psychology questionnaire | 257–67
  blocks | 8
  essentials | 29–30
  experience | 30–2
  low risk | 122–3, 131, 209–18
  options campaign | 221–9
  paper | 49–50
  personality | 8
  ranges | 69
  reasons for | 3–4
  rules | 184–5
  signals | 167–8
  tips | 123–5
  trends | 69
  types | 84
Trend–Hunter | 181, 191
Trends | 61, 65, 120, 121
  following | 176–7
  indicators | 167
  and spikes | 151
  time frames | 69–70
  trading | 69–70, 151–2
  trending signals | 70
Triune brain | 21, 22–5, 79, 242–3

TT1 240
TT2 240
TTT 47, 181, 239
  article 132–5
  consultancy 240
  contact details 240
  hotline 239–40
  Money Management services 240
  seminars 240
  systems 240
  technical analysis software 240
  TTT weekly system 74

Useful lies 31

V 190
Value 130–1, 134–5, 165, 176
van Goetzen, Richard 135

Williams, Bill 21, 22
  brain model 22–5
  chaos theory 22

XXX 190
You 4, 29-32

Zero sum 196–7